This Belongs to:
Nicole M. Fernandes

Out of the Blue

Harcourt Brace & Company

OUT OF THE BLUE

Senior Authors

Roger C. Farr

Dorothy S. Strickland

Authors

Richard F. Abrahamson ♦ Alma Flor Ada ♦ Barbara Bowen Coulter

Bernice E. Cullinan ♦ Margaret A. Gallego

W. Dorsey Hammond

Nancy Roser ♦ Junko Yokota ♦ Hallie Kay Yopp

Senior Consultant

Asa G. Hilliard III

Consultants

V. Kanani Choy ♦ Lee Bennett Hopkins ♦ Stephen Krashen ♦ Rosalia Salinas

Harcourt Brace & Company

Orlando Atlanta Austin Boston San Francisco Chicago Dallas New York Toronto London

Requests for permission to make copies of any part of the work should be mailed to: Permissions Department, Harcourt Brace & Company, 6277 Sea Harbor Drive, Orlando, Florida 32887-6777.

HARCOURT BRACE and Quill Design is a registered trademark of Harcourt Brace & Company.

Acknowledgments appear in the back of this work.

Printed in the United States of America

ISBN 0-15-306399-8

2 3 4 5 6 7 8 9 10   048   99 98 97

Dear Reader,

Have you ever heard of something coming "out of the blue"? A thing that comes out of the blue can be a surprise, and we have lots of surprises for you as you make your way through **Out of the Blue**.

You'll read about friends who live in cities, towns, and places in between. You'll meet people who make friends with animals, and animals who share tips for staying healthy. You'll discover stories that have been told in Laos, Africa, Puerto Rico, and the American Southwest for years and years. So, open your book and see what comes out of the blue!

Sincerely,

The Authors

The Authors

Celebrate Me!

CONTENTS

13 Theme
Opener

16 Bookshelf

Rhyming Nonfiction/Social Studies
18 This Is the Way We
Go to School
by Edith Baer
illustrated by Steve Björkman

Author and Illustrator Features:
Edith Baer and Steve Björkman

Poem
38 We Have a New Girl
in Class
by Aliki

Poem
39 How Do You Feel?
by Aliki

Photo Essay/Social Studies
42 What's for Lunch?
by Samantha Bonar
from 3-2-1 Contact

Realistic Fiction/Social Studies
44 Emily and Alice Again
by Joyce Champion
illustrated by Suçie Stevenson

Author and Illustrator Features:
Joyce Champion and Suçie Stevenson

Art
Art and Literature:
64 *Ronde des Enfants*
by Pablo Picasso

Realistic Fiction/Music
66 Max Found Two Sticks
written and illustrated by
Brian Pinkney

Author Feature: Brian Pinkney

Nonfiction/Music
94 Balloon Tom-Tom
by Eddie Herschel Oates

Nonfiction/Health
96 Dinosaurs Alive
and Well!
by Laurie Krasny Brown
and Marc Brown

Author and Illustrator Features:
Laurie Krasny Brown and
Marc Brown

120 Theme
Wrap-Up

WE BELONG TOGETHER

CONTENTS

121 Theme
Opener

124 Bookshelf

Realistic Fiction/Social Studies
126 Matthew and Tilly
by Rebecca C. Jones
illustrated by Beth Peck

Author and Illustrator Features:
Rebecca C. Jones and Beth Peck

Poem
146 Two Friends
by Nikki Giovanni

Nonfiction/Social Studies
150 Hopscotch Around
the World
by Mary D. Lankford

Art
156 Art and Literature:
Two Young Girls
at the Piano
by Pierre Auguste Renoir

Realistic Fiction/Social Studies
158 Mr. Putter and Tabby
Pour the Tea
by Cynthia Rylant
illustrated by Arthur Howard

Author and Illustrator Features:
Cynthia Rylant and
Arthur Howard

Realistic Fiction/Social Studies
182 Six-Dinner Sid
written and illustrated by
Inga Moore

Author Feature: Inga Moore

Nonfiction/Health
202 Rosie the Visiting Dog
by Stephanie Calmenson
from Sesame Street® Magazine

Fantasy/Social Studies
204 Abuela
by Arthur Dorros
illustrated by Elisa Kleven

Author and Illustrator Features:
Arthur Dorros and Elisa Kleven

228 Theme
Wrap-Up

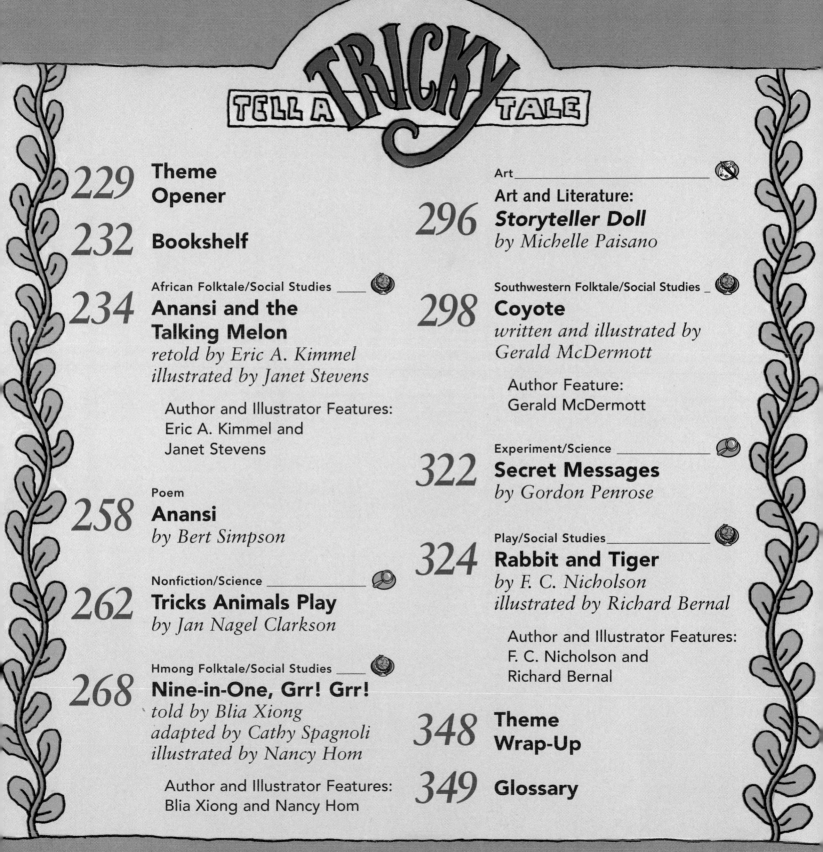

TELL A TRICKY TALE

229 **Theme Opener**

232 **Bookshelf**

African Folktale/Social Studies

234 **Anansi and the Talking Melon**
retold by Eric A. Kimmel
illustrated by Janet Stevens

Author and Illustrator Features:
Eric A. Kimmel and
Janet Stevens

Poem

258 **Anansi**
by Bert Simpson

Nonfiction/Science

262 **Tricks Animals Play**
by Jan Nagel Clarkson

Hmong Folktale/Social Studies

268 **Nine-in-One, Grr! Grr!**
told by Blia Xiong
adapted by Cathy Spagnoli
illustrated by Nancy Hom

Author and Illustrator Features:
Blia Xiong and Nancy Hom

Art

Art and Literature:
296 **Storyteller Doll**
by Michelle Paisano

Southwestern Folktale/Social Studies

298 **Coyote**
written and illustrated by
Gerald McDermott

Author Feature:
Gerald McDermott

Experiment/Science

322 **Secret Messages**
by Gordon Penrose

Play/Social Studies

324 **Rabbit and Tiger**
by F. C. Nicholson
illustrated by Richard Bernal

Author and Illustrator Features:
F. C. Nicholson and
Richard Bernal

348 **Theme Wrap-Up**

349 **Glossary**

Celebrate Me!

Has anyone ever told you that you're special? Well, you are! Maybe you are a good friend. Maybe you know how to make people laugh. There could be something else that you do well. Everyone is special in some way. And that's what makes life interesting!

Celebrate

Me!

Contents

This Is the Way We Go to School
by Edith Baer

We Have a New Girl in Class
How Do You Feel?
written and illustrated by Aliki

What's for Lunch?
by Samantha Bonar

Emily and Alice Again
by Joyce Champion

Art and Literature:
Ronde des Enfants
by Pablo Picasso

Max Found Two Sticks
written and illustrated
by Brian Pinkney

Balloon Tom-Tom
by Eddie Herschel Oates

Dinosaurs Alive and Well!
by Laurie Krasny Brown
and Marc Brown

Bookshelf

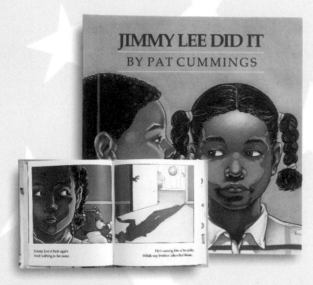

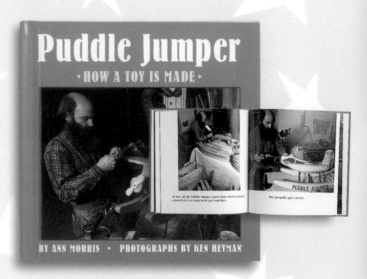

Jimmy Lee Did It

written and illustrated
by Pat Cummings

When things go wrong, Artie blames someone called Jimmy Lee. Artie's sister Angel tries to catch Jimmy Lee in the act. Can she do it?

Signatures Library
Award-Winning Author

Puddle Jumper: How a Toy Is Made

by Ann Morris

Sarah helps her dad make a puddle jumper. What is it? How is it made? You'll soon find out!

Signatures Library
Award-Winning Author

16

Emily and Alice
by Joyce Champion

Emily and Alice learn that it isn't always easy to be best friends.

Award-Winning Illustrator

Edward the Emu
by Sheena Knowles

Edward the emu visits other animals in the zoo to see what they are like.

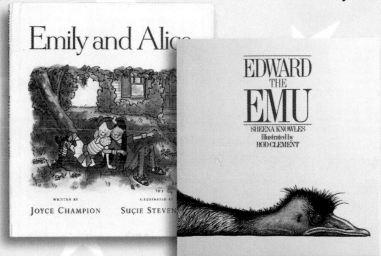

Lionel at Large
by Stephen Krensky

Every day is different for Lionel, and he makes the best of it.

Award-Winning Author

This Is the
Go to

by Edith Baer

This Is the Way We Go to School

A Book About Children Around the World

by EDITH BAER

Illustrated by STEVE BJÖRKMAN

Notable Trade Book in Social Studies

Way We School

illustrated by Steve Björkman

One by one or two by two—
Come along, it's fun to do!

Ellen takes it nice and slow,
time to watch the flowers grow.

Liz and Larry, as a rule,
wear their jogging shoes to school.

But at twenty minutes past,
roller skates are twice as fast.

21

And the fastest way by far
is by school bus or by car!

Jenny, Jerry, Pete, and Perry
ride the Staten Island Ferry.

23

Cable cars take Jack and Jill
up the hill—

and down the hill.

24

Michael and his friend Miguel
see the rooftops from the El.

25

Horse-and-buggy rides,
   it's plain,
start the day for
   Jake and Jane.

And in Philly, Mitch and Molly
go to school by trackless trolley!

Bianca, Beppo, Benedetto
ride aboard the *vaporetto*.

Bundled up
   against the breeze,
Niels and Solveig
   go on skis.

27

Palm trees help keep Ahmed cool
on his sunny walk to school.

Mira takes
    time out to play,
school's a hop
    and skip away.

And watch Sepp
and Heidi sail
through the air
from peak to vale!

Akinyi leaves
for school by train,
far across
the mountain chain.

29

Kay and Fay and Flo and Joe
go to school by radio.

Bicycles bring
Mei and Ling
through the traffic
of Nanjing.

30

And beneath the dripping sky,
Ram is riding high and dry.

William comes
ashore by boat,
counting sea gulls
while afloat.

Luz prefers the countryside.

Carlos takes the town in stride.

And the famous Metro line
suits Igor and Ilyana fine.

Go by Copter?
    By Skidoo?
Somewhere, sometimes,
    some kids do!
You come, too!
We'll look for you.

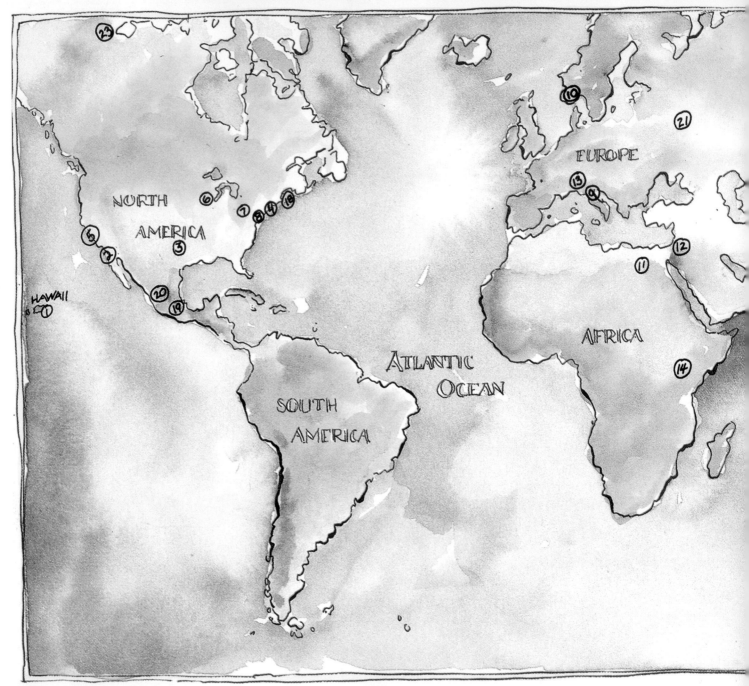

(1)	Ellen	(7)	Jake and Jane
(2)	Liz and Larry and the skater	(8)	Mitch and Molly
(3)	The bus and car riders	(9)	Bianca, Beppo, and Benedetto
(4)	Jenny, Jerry, Pete, and Perry	(10)	Niels and Solveig
(5)	Jack and Jill	(11)	Ahmed
(6)	Michael and Miguel	(12)	Mira

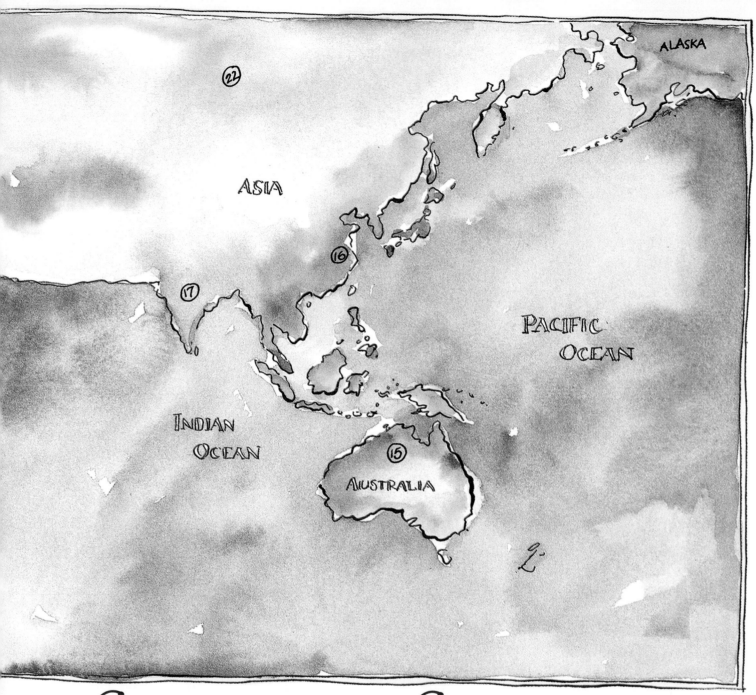

ALASKA

ASIA

PACIFIC OCEAN

INDIAN OCEAN

AUSTRALIA

13 Sepp and Heidi
14 Akinyi
15 Kay, Fay, Flo, and Joe
16 Mei and Ling
17 Ram
18 William

19 Carlos
20 Luz
21 Igor and Ilyana
22 The Copter passengers
23 The Skidoo passengers

This Is Where We Live

Ellen lives in Hawaii, U.S.A.

Liz and Larry and the skater live in California, U.S.A.

The bus and car riders live in Raytown, Missouri, U.S.A.

Jenny, Jerry, Pete, and Perry live in Staten Island, New York, U.S.A.

Jack and Jill live in San Francisco, California, U.S.A.

Michael and Miguel live in Chicago, Illinois, U.S.A.

Jake and Jane live in Lancaster, Pennsylvania, U.S.A.

Mitch and Molly live in Philadelphia, Pennsylvania, U.S.A.

Bianca, Beppo, and Benedetto live in Venice, Italy.

Niels and Solveig live in Norway.

Ahmed lives in Egypt.

Mira lives in Israel.

Sepp and Heidi live in Switzerland.

Akinyi lives in Kenya.

Kay, Fay, Flo, and Joe live in Australia.

Mei and Ling live in China.

Ram lives in India.

William lives in Maine, U.S.A.

Carlos and Luz live in Mexico.

Igor and Ilyana live in Moscow, Russia.

The Copter passengers live in Siberia, Russia.

The Skidoo passengers live in Canada.

Edith Baer   Passport

Name: Edith Baer

Place of Birth: Germany

Childhood: Edith came to the United States alone when she was only a teenager. She left Germany during World War II.

School: She worked hard all day and went to school at night.

Family: Married. She has two children and two grandchildren.

Job: Edith Baer is an author and a college writing teacher. She writes books, magazine stories, and poems. People all over the world read her work.

Steve Björkman   Passport

Name: Steve Björkman

Address: California

Family: Married. He has three children.

Job: He used to draw pictures for ads and greeting cards. Now he draws pictures for children's books. *This Is the Way We Go to School* is one of the first books that he has done.

Other: Steve liked drawing pictures for cards. It gave him practice drawing lots of people, animals, and places. This helped him when he started to draw pictures for children's books.

We Have a New Girl in Class

by Aliki

I'd like to hide. They're all staring at me. Is she laughing at me? I wish

I could fall through the crack in the floor...

she looks nice.

You'd feel shy, too, if you were standing up there.

she looks shy.

Hello. My name is Patricia.

39

Response Corner

Off We Go!

Make up a song about going to school.

1. Work as a whole group. Make a chart to show how the children in the story travel to school. Add your ideas to the chart.

Land	Sea	Air
walk	ferry	ski lift
jog	vaporetto	helicopter
roller skates		

2. Work with a small group. Make up a song about how you go to school. You can use a tune you know, like "London Bridge." Use the chart for ideas.

We can ride on roller skates, roller skates, roller skates. We can ride on roller skates, all the way to school.

40

How Would You Go?

1. Choose a child from the story who you would like to meet. Make it someone who travels to school in a different way than you do.

2. Draw a picture of the two of you traveling to school together.

3. On another sheet of paper, write about why this would be fun.

   After you finish, you can add your pages to a class book.

What Do You Think?

- What did you learn from this story that you never thought about before?
- Which way of going to school was most interesting to you? Why?

41

What's for Lunch?

Kids Chow Down Around the World

by **Samantha Bonar**

Kids in India eat with their right hands only. The rims of the steel plates help scoop up food.

Sukhi Bhaji (dry vegetables) with poori (bread) and hot mango pickle.

Want a bite of sushi? This roll has avocado, rice, and fish eggs!

Lunch for Japanese kids isn't in the bag— it's in the obento!

What's for lunch? Cold rice with sesame seeds, fried goodies, vegetable salad, and fresh fruit.

This chiko roll is like an egg roll.

Chips ahoy! Some kids like salt and vinegar crisps best.

Australian kids eat up meat pies—beef and sauce baked in a pastry crust.

Emily and Alice Again

Award-Winning
Illustrator

WRITTEN BY
JOYCE CHAMPION

ILLUSTRATED BY
SUÇIE STEVENSON

44

The Trade

Emily ran over to her best friend Alice's house. "*Oooh,* Alice, where did you get those cool sunglasses?" she asked.

"My grandma sent them to me from Florida," said Alice. "Here, you can try them on."

Emily tried on Alice's new sunglasses. She looked up at the sky. She looked down at the ground. Everything looked pink and happy.

"I *love* these sunglasses," said Emily. "I could wear them forever." At that moment she knew she had to have them.

Alice watched Emily suspiciously. "I want my sunglasses back now," she said.

Emily gave Alice her sunglasses. But she had a plan. "Don't move," she told Alice. "I'll be right back."

Emily ran to her house. She came back to Alice's holding two stuffed animals. "Want to trade Zippidy and Doodah for your new sunglasses?" she asked.

"Don't you have your own sunglasses?" asked Alice.

"I only have the plain round kind," answered Emily. "I don't have cool heart-shaped glasses like yours. I don't have sunglasses that make the world pink and happy. Let's trade."

Alice looked at Emily's bears and shook her head. "Sorry, Emily," she said. "No trade."

"I'll be right back," said Emily.

Emily returned to Alice's holding a box. "I'll trade you my favorite rocks," she said, "even all the sparkly ones, if I can have your sunglasses."

Alice looked at Emily's rock collection and shook her head. "Sorry, Emily," she said. "Still no trade."

"OK," said Emily, "wait here—because I'll be back."

Emily ran to her house again. She *had* to find something to trade. She walked in circles around her room. Then she saw her little sister, Nora, in the doorway. This was her best idea yet!

Emily grabbed her sister's hand and ran back to Alice's.

"Alice," she said, "I'll trade my favorite sister—my *only* sister—for your new sunglasses."

Alice looked at Nora. She looked at her chubby little legs and tiny red sneakers. Alice nodded. "OK, I'll trade!"

Alice gave Emily her new sunglasses. Emily gave Alice her only sister.

Emily ran home and put on her new sunglasses. Everything looked pink and happy. "I am a beautiful movie star," she said to the mirror. Then she ran out back.

Emily lay on a beach chair. She looked up at the pink sun. She watched pink clouds float by. "I am on a big cruise ship," she said to the sky. "Soon I will be on a faraway island."

Emily heard giggles coming from Alice's backyard.
She could see that Alice was teaching Nora how to do
cartwheels. *I'm glad they're having fun,* she thought.

Emily polished her sunglasses. She looked over at Alice's yard again. She watched Alice put on a puppet show for Nora. She watched Alice give Nora horseback rides. She heard Nora laugh and shriek. *They're REALLY having fun,* thought Emily.

Emily put her sunglasses on. She looked up at the sky.
She looked down at the ground. The world was still pink.
But it didn't seem quite so happy.

Emily yanked off the glasses and ran next door. "Alice," she said, "I think I've had enough fun with your cool sunglasses."

Alice tried to catch her breath. "I think I've had enough fun with your sister," she said.

Emily gave back Alice's sunglasses. Alice waved good-bye to Nora.

"Let's just *borrow* next time, OK?" asked Alice.

"Good idea," said Emily.

Alice smiled and put on her sunglasses.

Emily smiled as she and Nora cartwheeled home.

JOYCE CHAMPION

Are Emily and Alice like any people you know?
Emily is like me. Alice is like my best friend when I was growing up. She lived in the apartment next door to my family.

Are you still friends with her?
Yes. She was even in my wedding.

Did you really trade your sunglasses for your little sister? Not really, but I did trade my mother for a doll.

You did? To Alice?
No. Another friend who had a neat doll was at my house. I traded, and my mother went along with it. My mother and my friend had such a good time that I made her trade back. *Joyce Champion*

SUÇIE STEVENSON

Suçie Stevenson has been writing children's books and drawing pictures for them for many years. One way that this artist gets ideas for her art is to think about the big family she grew up in. When she made the pictures for this story, she used her memories of the things she and her sister used to do together.

Another way that Suçie Stevenson gets ideas for her art is to go to the beautiful seashore on Cape Cod in Massachusetts. She loves it there! That's where she lives with her two Labrador retrievers.

Suçie Stevenson

MAKE SUNGLASSES

Cool-Looking Shades

Just like Emily and Alice, everyone wants a pair of cool

sunglasses to wear. You can make a pair!

1. Cut out two joined cups from an egg carton.

2. Cut a hole in the bottom of each cup.

3. Cut out a triangle between the two cups to

fit over your nose.

4. Staple a pipe cleaner to each side of the glasses.

    5. Decorate your glasses.

Then act out your favorite part of the story

with a partner.

You will need:
egg carton
scissors
markers
decorations
glue
pipe cleaners
stapler

TRADE GOODS

Let's Trade!

Did you ever trade something with a friend? Talk about how you know if a trade is fair. Then make a beautiful bookmark. Plan a trading day. Trade the bookmarks you have made. After trading, talk about what you learned.

To make your bookmark, you might want to use:

construction paper
hole punch
stamp pads
scissors
glue
rubber stamps
markers and crayons
stickers
yarn

What Do You Think?

- What did Emily and Alice learn about trading?
- What part of the story did you like best? Why?

63

Art & Literature

What are the children in this painting doing? Would you like to play with them? What might they be celebrating?

Ronde des Enfants
by Pablo Picasso

Pablo Picasso was a famous Spanish artist. He painted this picture when he was 19 years old. The title is French and means "children's dance." In this kind of dance, children move in a circle and sing. How does Picasso show you that these girls are moving?

65

MAX FOUND TWO STICKS

BY BRIAN PINKNEY

MAX FOUND
Two Sticks

BRIAN PINKNEY

Award-Winning
Author

It was a day when Max didn't feel like talking to anyone. He just sat on his front steps and watched the clouds gather in the sky.

A strong breeze shook the tree in front
of his house, and Max saw two heavy
twigs fall to the ground.

"What are you gonna do with those sticks?" Max's grandpa asked as he washed the front windows.

Not saying a word, Max tapped on his thighs, *Pat . . . pat-tat.*

Putter-putter . . . pat-tat.
His rhythm imitated the sound of
the pigeons, startled into flight.

71

When Max's mother came home carrying new hats for his twin sisters, she asked, "What are you doing with Grandpa's cleaning bucket, Son?"

Max responded by patting the bucket, *Tap-tap-tap*.

73

Tippy-tip . . . tat-tat. He created the rhythm of
the light rain falling against the front windows.

After a while the clouds moved on and the sun appeared. Cindy, Shaun and Jamal showed up drinking sodas. "Hey, Max! Whatcha doin' with those hatboxes?"

Again Max didn't answer. He just played on the boxes, *Dum . . . dum-de-dum.*

Di-di-di-di. Dum-dum.
Max drummed the beat of the tom-toms in a marching band.

"What are you up to with those soda bottles?" his dad asked as he brought out the garbage cans on his way to work.

Max answered on the bottles,
Dong . . . dang . . . dung.

Ding . . . dong . . . ding! His music joined the chiming of the bells in the church around the corner.

Soon the twins came out to show off
their new hats. "Hey, Max," they asked,
"what are you doin' with those garbage cans?"

Max hammered out a reply on the cans,
Cling . . . clang . . . da-BANG!

A-cling-clang . . . DA-BANGGGG!
Max pounded out the sound of the wheels
thundering down the tracks under the train
on which his father worked as a conductor.

Suddenly Max heard *Thump-di-di-thump* . . . *THUMP-DI-DI-THUMP!* as a marching band rounded the corner.

Max watched the drummers with amazement
as they passed, copying their rhythms. The last
drummer saw Max. Then with a nod and a wink,
he tossed Max his spare set of sticks.

"Thanks," called Max—and he didn't miss a beat.

BRIAN PINKNEY

What made you decide to write this book?
I wanted to write a book about drumming because I've been a drummer most of my life. I almost made music my career. But even though I had the idea, I didn't really have a story. I would jot down notes about a boy and how he liked to drum.

It took me about four years to finish the book. I decided to start with the pictures. I would draw a little, then write a little. Most of the words came to me when I was just waking up in the morning or when I was away from my studio.

91

RESPONSE CORNER

EXPERIMENT WITH RHYTHM

MAKE YOUR OWN MUSIC

Max found out that he could make music using only two sticks. What kind of rubbing, clapping, clicking, and snapping rhythms can you make without using instruments?

Work with a partner. Make your own music. Then teach your rhythm to others. Try adding words to your rhythm.

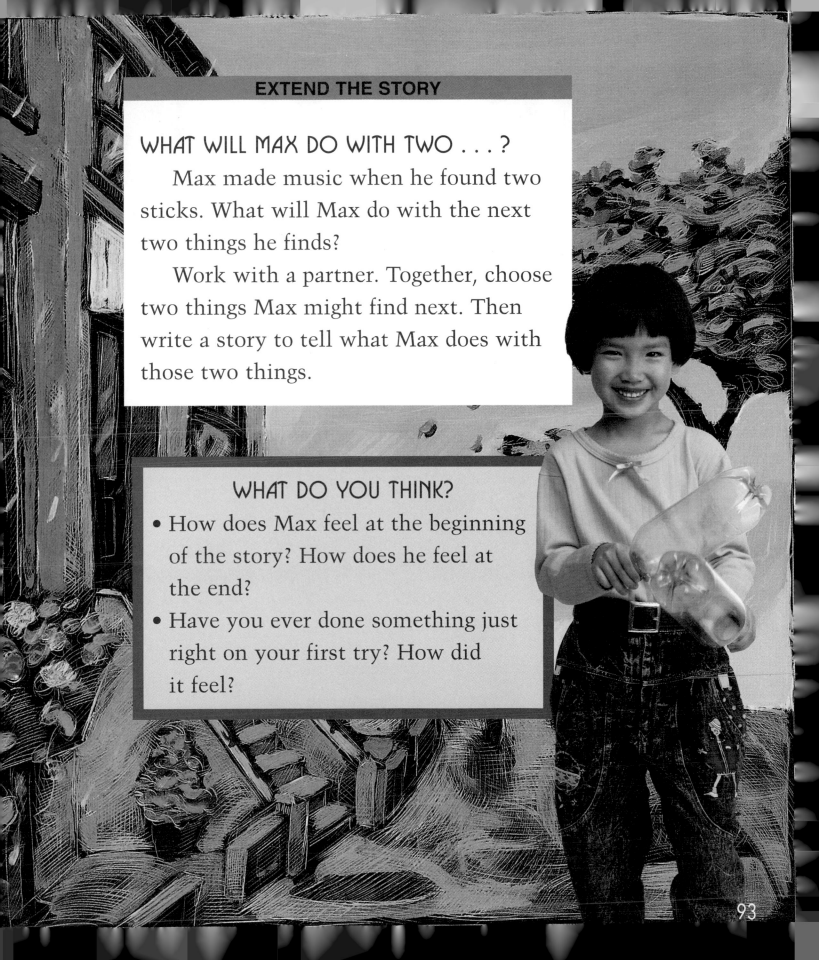

WHAT WILL MAX DO WITH TWO . . . ?

Max made music when he found two sticks. What will Max do with the next two things he finds?

Work with a partner. Together, choose two things Max might find next. Then write a story to tell what Max does with those two things.

WHAT DO YOU THINK?

- How does Max feel at the beginning of the story? How does he feel at the end?
- Have you ever done something just right on your first try? How did it feel?

93

Balloon Tom-Tom

by Eddie Herschel Oates • illustrated by Michael Koelsch

Materials needed:

EMPTY JUICE CAN,

OATMEAL BOX,

POTATO-CHIP CAN, or

other cylindrical container

CAN OPENER

SCISSORS

2 LARGE BALLOONS

2 HEAVY RUBBER BANDS

2 PENCILS (with erasers)

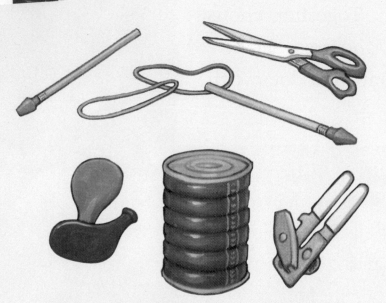

Putting it together:

1. If your container is open at only one end, use scissors or a can opener to open the other end of the container. This is the drum body.

2. Cut the open end off a large balloon.

94

3. Stretch the closed end of the balloon over one end of the drum body. The balloon is the drum skin.

4. Hold the balloon in place with a heavy rubber band and smooth out all the wrinkles to make the skin tight.

5. Repeat steps 2 to 4 on the other end of the drum body.

Now it's time to play your tom-tom. Pencils with erasers make great drumsticks, or use your fingers. Strike the skin around the rim or in the center to make different sounds. BOOM-BOOM-BOOM, RAP, RAP, RAP, BOOM-BOOM—and off you go!

95

DINOSAURS
ALIVE AND WELL!
◆ A Guide to Good Health ◆
Laurie Krasny Brown ◆ Marc Brown

Award-Winning
Author
Award-Winning
Illustrator

DINO

SAURS ALIVE AND WELL!

by Laurie Krasny Brown
illustrated by Marc Brown

Take Care of Yourself

There's just one you.

That makes you special.

There's a lot you can do to take care of yourself and become the healthiest, happiest person you can be!

Taking care of yourself means treating yourself well every single day—looking out for your body, your mind, and your spirit.

Exercise Your Body

Exercising every day helps your body stay healthy. When you exercise, your body works harder, your heartbeat is stronger, and you can feel your pulse go faster. Even though it takes energy to exercise, getting exercise helps you feel *more* energetic.

Some exercises make you stronger. Muscles that get no exercise become weak and flabby. They may even shrink in size.

Other exercises help your body stay flexible.

And, the more you exercise, the longer you'll be able to play without getting tired.

There are many different games and sports. The only way to find out which ones you like is to try them!

Some sports take lots of practice. Try to remember: you don't have to be perfect at a sport to have fun.

Everyone's body is different. Don't worry about what yours can't do— be proud of what you *can* do!

Exercise Your Mind

Your body isn't all that needs exercise—so does your mind. Every time you pretend, make decisions, figure something out, or learn something new, you're exercising your mind. It doesn't happen only in school!

Believe in yourself! Expecting that you can do something is often half the battle.

You may want to do things the same way your friends do, but it's good to think for yourself, too.

Always doing the same thing can put your mind to sleep.

Everyone is good at something. Trying different activities helps you discover your own special talents.

Deal with Your Feelings

Feelings aren't right or wrong—they just are. Sometimes we all feel . . .

mad

sad

scared

glad

Letting out your feelings is healthier than keeping them to yourself.

Don't sit and stew. Anger gives you energy to do all kinds of things!

mad

If you feel sad, crying helps you feel better.

sad

Sharing your scared feelings with someone you trust can help you feel less alone.

This test will be **so** hard!

I know it.

scared

Be proud of yourself when you do something well.

Mom, look! I won!

glad

Solving problems isn't always easy. But most problems can be solved if you look them right in the eye. And you'll usually feel better in the end.

mad

Try to think up fair ways to settle arguments.

sad

You can make a new friend
after you lose an old one—
when you're ready.

It takes courage to admit you're scared. But someone
else's help may be just what you need.

scared

Mrs. Silver, can you
help me?

Take It Easy

Remember that you don't always have to be busy.
Give yourself time to daydream and be by yourself.

Be a Friend, Have a Friend

There's nothing like a good friend to make you feel happy.

Being a friend means a lot of sharing.

Friends stick together through good and bad.

Give yourself time to get to know new friends—and give them time to get to know you.

Friends often like to do the same things or go to the same places.

But sometimes even friends want to do something different or to be by themselves. That's okay, too.

Because friends like each other just the way they are!

Now that you know how to take care of yourself, you can help take care of others, too. You're part of the world of living things, each one special and unique . . . just like you!

LAURIE KRASNY BROWN

Dear Reader,

I've written a lot of books, but *Dinosaurs Alive and Well!* is extra special to me. You see, I wrote the words and my husband, Marc Brown, drew the pictures.

Whenever I start to write a book, I read all I can on the subject. Next, I make a list of what I need to put in the book. Then, I write and rewrite.

When I am done, I get someone who knows a lot about what's in the book to read it. One expert who looked at this book said that being healthy is more than just taking care of your body. It's taking care of your spirit, too. I really liked that idea.

Your friend,

Laurie Krasny Brown

MARC BROWN

Dear Reader,

Many kids know my artwork from my Arthur books, but I like to do information books, too. I have done several books using these dinosaur characters. I chose to draw dinosaurs because they are powerful animals and I want my readers to feel powerful. I am proud of these books because I think they help kids feel good about themselves.

When I was young, I spent most of my time drawing. After my grandmother took me to an art museum, I became interested in painting. My three children are also interested in art. Today, when I'm not working, I like to spend time gardening. My wife, Laurie, and I grow flowers, fruits, and vegetables.

Your friend,

Marc Brown

RESPONSE CORNER

Fun Fitness!

You know that exercise keeps you feeling good. Work with a group to make up your own exercise moves.

1. Decide which exercises to do.
2. Choose the best music.
3. Practice your moves.

Then you can teach your exercise moves to another group.

Pass on the News with Puppets!

The tips in "Dinosaurs Alive and Well!" are important to remember. Work with a small group. Choose a tip from the story that you think is important. Make puppets and plan a short play about the tip. Put on your puppet play for another class. Share what you learned about staying healthy.

To make dinosaur stick puppets:

1. Draw and cut out a dinosaur shape.
2. Tape the shape to a stick to make a handle.

What Do You Think?

- What are three things you can do to stay healthy?
- What have you learned about staying healthy that you did not know before?

Wrap-Up

People may do some things differently, but each one of us has something special to share.

- Max, Emily, and Alice all tried something new. What did each character learn about himself or herself?
- What advice might the dinosaurs in "Dinosaurs Alive and Well!" give to Emily and Alice? What might they say to Max? Explain your answers.

Activity Corner

Think about something that you have learned. It could be a new thing that you have tried, like riding a bike. Draw a picture of yourself doing that thing. Write sentences that tell about your picture. Celebrate what you learned!

WE BELONG TOGETHER

Having special people in your life can make you happy. Families, friends, pets, and others cheer you up when you're sad. They celebrate with you when you're happy. Whether your special ones are old or young, and whether they live with you or far away, they make the world a better place.

Theme

WE BELONG TOGETHER

CONTENTS

Matthew and Tilly

by Rebecca C. Jones

Two Friends

by Nikki Giovanni

Hopscotch Around the World

by Mary D. Lankford

Art and Literature:
Two Young Girls at the Piano

by Pierre Auguste Renoir

Mr. Putter and Tabby Pour the Tea

by Cynthia Rylant

Six-Dinner Sid

written and illustrated by Inga Moore

Rosie the Visiting Dog

by Stephanie Calmenson

Abuela

by Arthur Dorros

BOOKSHELF

There's a Dragon in My Sleeping Bag

by James Howe

Alex feels left out when his brother Simon spends time with a make-believe friend— a dragon. Then Alex discovers a make-believe friend, too!

Signatures Library
Award-Winning Author

Mary Ann

written and illustrated by Betsy James

When Amy's best friend moves away, Amy finds a new friend— an insect!

Signatures Library
SLJ Best Books

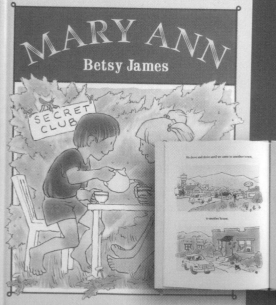

124

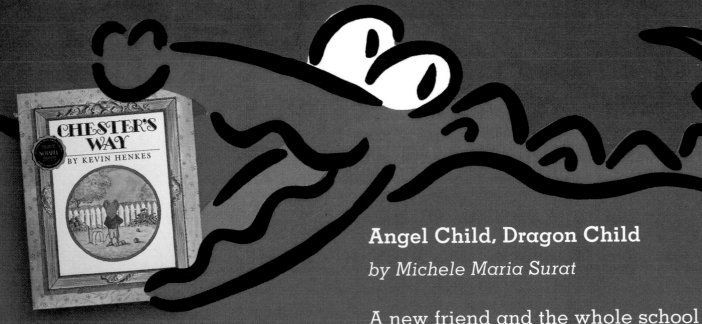

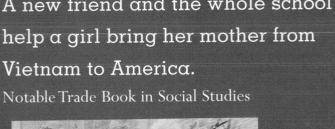

Chester's Way

by Kevin Henkes

Chester and Wilson like to do things their way. But things change when they meet Lilly.

ALA Notable Book

Angel Child, Dragon Child

by Michele Maria Surat

A new friend and the whole school help a girl bring her mother from Vietnam to America.

Notable Trade Book in Social Studies

Polka and Dot

by Dena Schutzer

A lonely bird flies near and far to find her best friend.

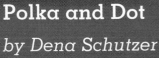

125

MATTHEW
AND
TILLY

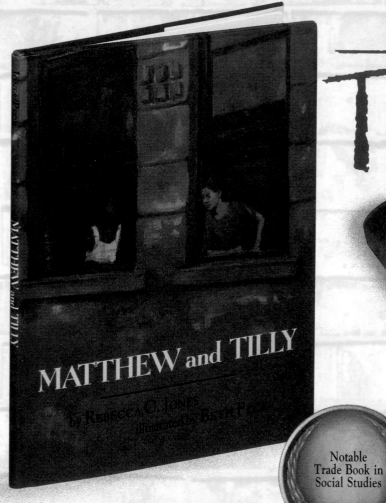

by Rebecca C. Jones
illustrated by Beth Peck

Notable
Trade Book in
Social Studies

MATTHEW and TILLY
were friends.

They rode bikes together,

and they played hide-and-seek together.

They sold lemonade together. When business was slow, they played sidewalk games together.

And sometimes they ate ice-cream cones together.

Once they even rescued a lady's kitten from a tree together.
The lady gave them money for the bubble-gum machines.
So later they chewed gum together and remembered how brave
they had been.

Sometimes, though, Matthew and Tilly got sick of each other.
One day when they were coloring, Matthew broke Tilly's
purple crayon. He didn't mean to, but he did.

"You broke my crayon," Tilly said in her crabbiest voice.

"It was an old crayon," Matthew said in his grouchiest voice. "It was ready to break."

"No, it wasn't," Tilly said. "It was a brand-new crayon, and you broke it. You always break everything."

"Stop being so picky," Matthew said. "You're always so picky and stinky and mean."

"Well, you're so stupid," Tilly said. "You're so stupid and stinky and mean."

Matthew stomped up the stairs. By himself.

Tilly found a piece of chalk and began drawing numbers and squares on the sidewalk. By herself.

Upstairs, Matthew got out his cash register and some cans so he could play store. He piled the cans extra high, and he put prices on everything. This was the best store he had ever made. Probably because that picky and stinky and mean old Tilly wasn't around to mess it up.

But he didn't have a customer. And playing store wasn't much fun without a customer.

Tilly finished drawing the numbers and squares. She drew them really big, with lots of squiggly lines. This was the best sidewalk game she had ever drawn. Probably because that stupid and stinky and mean old Matthew wasn't around to mess it up.

But she didn't have anyone to play with. And a sidewalk game wasn't much fun without another player.

Matthew looked out the window and wondered what Tilly was doing. Tilly looked up at Matthew's window and wondered what he was doing.

She smiled, just a little. That was enough for Matthew.

"I'm sorry," he called.

"So am I," said Tilly.

And Matthew ran
downstairs so they
could play.

142

Together again.

REBECCA C. JONES

When Rebecca Jones was young, she had a friend named Larry. They used to argue all the time. That's what gave Rebecca Jones the idea for this story.

One time, she and Larry got lost when they took a walk. After a while, they found their way home. When they got to Rebecca Jones's house, there were police cars parked outside. They ran inside to see what all the excitement was about. They soon found out that their parents had called the police because *they* were missing.

Rebecca Jones moved when she was seven and never saw Larry again. She wishes that he could read this story and know that she wrote it about the two of them.

BETH PECK

Beth Peck decided to draw Matthew and Tilly in a place she knows very well. The pictures in the book are based on Beth's childhood home, a busy neighborhood in New York City. The book's apartment buildings, stores, signs, iron gates, sidewalks, and fire hydrants look a lot like what Beth Peck saw every day as a young girl.

STATIONERY

HOUSEW

Beth Peck

Rebecca C. Jones

145

TWO FRIENDS

lydia and shirley have
two pierced ears and
two bare ones
five pigtails
two pairs of sneakers
two berets
two smiles
one necklace
one bracelet
lots of stripes and
one good friendship

by Nikki Giovanni
photo by Joyce Sangirardi

RESPONSE CORNER

Do I Have a Surprise for You!

Matthew and Tilly liked doing things together. What do you think they might do to surprise each other?

1. Work with a partner. One can be Matthew and one can be Tilly.
2. Plan a surprise for the other character. Draw and write about it.
3. Give hints to help your partner guess the surprise.
4. Show it to your partner.

Make a class book with everyone's pages.

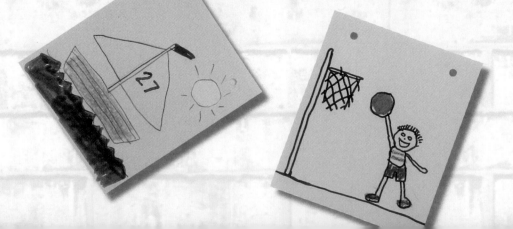

148

"All Smiles"

Make a smile you can eat!

When Matthew and Tilly were sharing and having fun, they were "all smiles." You and your friends can share a treat that will make you all smiles, too.

You will need:
- 4 friends
- 1 red apple cut into 8 slices
- peanut butter
- tiny marshmallows
- plastic knife
- napkins

To make each smile:
1. Spread peanut butter on one side of an apple slice.
2. Push marshmallows into the peanut butter.
3. Put another apple slice on top to finish the smile.

What Do You Think?

- What did Matthew and Tilly learn about friendship?
- How are Matthew and Tilly like you and your friends? How are they different?

HOPSCOTCH
Around the World

by
Mary D.
Lankford

PELE The island of Aruba in the Netherlands Antilles is just twenty miles north of the coast of Venezuela. Many of the trees on the island have been bent into unusual shapes by the strong winds that blow across the island. Because of these winds, an object that will not blow or roll away must be used as a puck. A stone or coin makes a good puck for the children of Aruba.

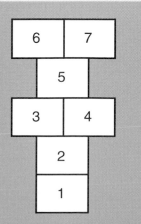

6	7

5

3	4

2

1

•ARUBA

VENEZUELA

W • • E

151

DIRECTIONS:

1. Throw the puck into box 1.

2. Hop into box 2. Then jump into boxes 3 and 4, putting one foot in each box.

3. Hop into box 5, and jump in boxes 6 and 7 just as you did for boxes 3 and 4.

4. Jump and turn, landing again in boxes 6 and 7, now facing the rest of the pattern.

5. Hop into box 5. Then jump into boxes 3 and 4, putting one foot in each box.

6. Hop into box 2, and pick up the puck from box 1. Hop out of the pattern without landing in box 1.

Step 1

Step 4

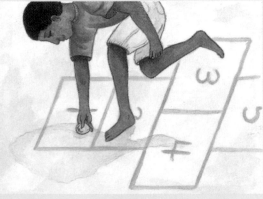

Step 6

7. Throw the puck into box 2, and repeat the entire pattern. If the puck lands in the wrong box or outside the pattern, you lose your turn.

Step 7

8. Throw the puck into box 3. Hop into boxes 1 and 2 and then into box 4. Continue through the pattern and, on the way back, pick up the puck from box 3 while balancing on one foot in box 4. Never hop into a box with a puck in it.

Step 8

9. If you step on a line, you also lose your turn, but your puck stays in place until you try again. Players cannot hop or jump into a box that holds either their own puck or that of another player.

10. The first player who completes the entire pattern wins the game.

ESCARGOT

Snails are a favorite food in France. The spiral shape of the shell of a snail (*escargot* in French) is the pattern used for one variation of hopscotch played there. Escargot is one of the few hopscotch games in which no puck is used. The game is also called La Marelle Ronde (round hopscotch).

DIRECTIONS:

1. Before you begin hopping, decide which foot you will hop on. If you decide on your left foot, you must hop in and out each time on that foot.

2. Hop through the snail.

3. Hop only once in each space. No player may touch a line when hopping.

4. In the center space, you may rest on both feet.

5. After resting, turn and hop back to the beginning. Repeat the pattern once more.

6. After you have hopped in and out twice, choose one space for your "house." Write your initials in this space. This becomes another rest space for you. No other player may hop into your house.

7. The game ends when it is impossible for anyone to hop into the center space or when all of the squares have initials in them. The player who "owns" the greatest number of squares wins.

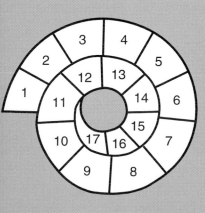

ART AND LITERATURE

Matthew and Tilly learned that friends should be together. Do you think the girls in the painting like being together? What might a painting of you and a good friend show?

Two Young Girls at the Piano
by Pierre Auguste Renoir

Artist Pierre Renoir lived and painted in France. He liked to show ways that people are special. What do you think he wanted to show about the girls in this painting?

157

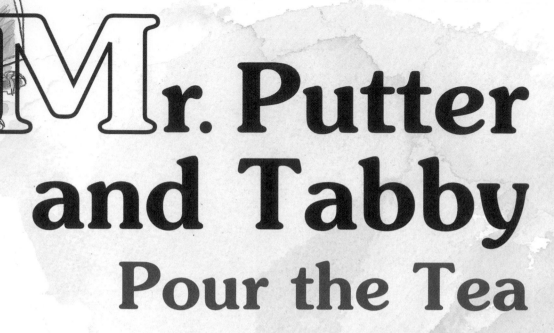

Mr. Putter and Tabby
Pour the Tea

Award-Winning Author

BY
CYNTHIA RYLANT
ILLUSTRATED BY
ARTHUR HOWARD

CYNTHIA RYLANT

Mr. Putter and Tabby
Pour the Tea

ILLUSTRAT
HU HOWA

Mr. Putter

Before he got his fine cat, Tabby,
Mr. Putter lived all alone.

In the mornings he had no one
to share his English muffins.
In the afternoons he had no
one to share his tea.
And in the evenings
there was no one
Mr. Putter could
tell his stories to.
And he had the
most wonderful
stories to tell.

161

All day long as Mr. Putter
clipped his roses
and fed his tulips
and watered his trees,
Mr. Putter wished for
some company.

He had warm muffins to eat.
He had good tea to pour.
And he had wonderful stories to tell.
Mr. Putter was tired of living alone.

Mr. Putter wanted a cat.

2

Tabby

Mr. Putter went to the pet
store. "Do you have cats?"
he asked the pet store lady.
"We have fourteen," she said.
Mr. Putter was delighted.
But when he looked into
the cage, he was not.

"These are kittens," he said.
"I was hoping for a cat."
"Oh, no one wants cats, sir,"
said the pet store lady.
"They are not cute.
They are not peppy."

Mr. Putter himself had not
been cute and peppy for
a very long time.
He said, "I want a cat."

"Then go to the shelter, sir,"
said the pet store lady.
"You are sure to find a cat."

Mr. Putter went to the shelter.

"Have you any cats?"
he asked the shelter man.
"We have a fat gray one,
a thin black one, and
an old yellow one," said the man.
"Did you say old?" asked Mr. Putter.

The shelter man brought
Mr. Putter the old yellow
cat. Its bones creaked,
its fur was thinning,
and it seemed a little
deaf. Mr. Putter creaked,
his hair was thinning,
and he was a little
deaf, too.

166

So he took the old yellow cat home.
He named her Tabby.
And that is how their life began.

3
Mr. Putter and Tabby

Tabby loved Mr. Putter's tulips.
She was old,
and beautiful things
meant more to her.

She would rub past all
the yellow tulips.
Then she would roll past
all the red tulips.

Then she would take her
bath among all the pink
tulips. Mr. Putter clipped
roses while Tabby bathed.

In the mornings
Mr. Putter and Tabby liked
to share an English muffin.
Mr. Putter ate his with jam.
Tabby ate hers with cream cheese.

In the afternoons
Mr. Putter and Tabby
liked to share tea.
Mr. Putter took his with sugar.
Tabby took hers with cream.

169

And in the evenings
they sat by the window,
and Mr. Putter told stories.
He told the most wonderful
stories. Each story made
Tabby purr.

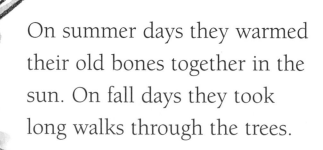

On summer days they warmed
their old bones together in the
sun. On fall days they took
long walks through the trees.

And on winter days they turned
the opera up *very* loud.

After a while it seemed as if
they had always lived together.

Tabby knew just what Mr. Putter
was going to do next.

Mr. Putter knew just where
Tabby was going to sleep next.

In the mornings each looked for the other as soon as they opened their eyes.

And at night each looked for the other as their eyes were closing. Mr. Putter could not remember life without Tabby.

PUTTER
& TABBY

176

Tabby could not remember
life without Mr. Putter.
They lived among their
tulips and trees.

They ate their muffins.

They poured their tea.

They turned up the opera,

and enjoyed the most perfect company of all—

each other.

CYNTHIA RYLANT

Dear friends and readers,

Hello! How do I introduce myself? I am the writer of many books about things like

having tea

petting kittens

 growing gardens

and all sorts of ordinary things.

I have a son who likes LOUD music and I have two good dogs and two sweet cats who like sunshine and food.

I think that life is full of beautiful things, beautiful small things and beautiful large things to celebrate. I celebrate them in my books. And I hope that you will celebrate with me.

♡ Cynthia Rylant

ARTHUR HOWARD

Dear readers,

I had fun drawing the pictures for this story. What would Mr. Putter's house look like? What kind of car would he drive? Hmmm . . .

The house was easy. It's my brother's house in New York. With its pointy roof and big front porch with a porch swing, it was perfect for Mr. Putter.

The car was a little harder to find. Then one day, I saw the perfect car parked on the street. It was old, but not too old, and it looked slow-moving—kind of like Mr. Putter.

A lot of people ask me if I have a cat. I love cats, but I don't have one. I have a pet hermit crab named Buster, though.

Your friend,

Arthur Howard

Response Corner

Perfect Company

Tabby was perfect company for Mr. Putter. Make a greeting card to give to the person or pet who is *your* perfect company.

To make your card:

1. Fold a piece of drawing paper in half.

2. On the top of the folded paper, draw the cover of your card.

3. Open the card and write a message to your perfect company. Write your name to show who made the card.

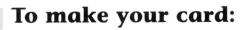

180

Mr. Putter's Family Album

Tabby and Mr. Putter are a family. They do everything together. Mr. Putter even has an album full of photos of the two of them.

Draw a new picture for Mr. Putter's family album. Write a sentence to tell what Mr. Putter and Tabby are doing together. Add your drawing to a class album.

What Do You Think?
- How are Mr. Putter and Tabby alike?
- Why do you think Mr. Putter and Tabby make a good team?

181

Six-Dinner Sid

by Inga Moore

Award-Winning
Author

Sid lived at number one Aristotle Street.

He also lived at number two, number three,
number four, number five, and number six.

Sid lived in six houses so that he could have
six dinners. Each night he would slip out
of number one, where he might have
had chicken, into number
two for fish . . .

on to number three for lamb

liver at number four

fish again at number five . . .

ending at number six with beef-and-kidney stew.

Since the neighbors did not talk to
each other on Aristotle Street, they
did not know what Sid was up to.
They all believed the cat
they fed was theirs, and
theirs alone.

But Sid had to work hard for his dinners. It wasn't easy being six people's pet. He had six different names to remember and six different ways to behave.

When he was being Scaramouche, Sid put on swanky airs.

As Bob he had a job.

He was naughty as Mischief . . .

and silly as Sally.

As Sooty he smooched . . .

but as Schwartz he had to act rough and tough.

All this work sometimes wore Sid out. But he didn't care, as long as he had his six dinners. And, besides, he liked being . . .

scratched in six different places . . .

and sleeping in six different beds.

In fact, life on Aristotle Street was just about
perfect for Sid, until . . .

one cold, damp day, he caught a nasty cough.

The next thing he knew, he was being taken
to the vet. Poor Sid, he was taken not once . . .

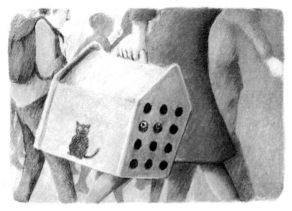

not twice . . .

but six times!

He went with six different people, in
six different ways.

The vet said Sid's cough wasn't
nearly as nasty as it sounded; but,
to be on the safe side, he should
have a spoonful of medicine.

Of course,
Sid didn't have just one spoonful
of medicine.

He had six!

Now, one black cat does look much like another; but nobody, not even a busy vet, could see the same cat six times without becoming suspicious. Sure enough, when he checked in his appointment book, the vet found six cats with a cough—all living on Aristotle Street!

So he called the owners at once . . .

and, oh dear, Sid was found out!
When they discovered what he had been up to,
Sid's owners said he had no business eating so
many dinners.

They said, in the future, they would make sure
he had only one dinner a day.

But Sid was a six-dinner-a-day cat. So he went to live at number one Pythagoras Place. He also went to live at numbers two, three, four, five, and six.

Unlike Aristotle Street, the people who lived on Pythagoras
Place talked to their neighbors. So, right from the start,
everyone knew about Sid's six dinners.

And, because everyone knew, nobody minded.

198

A Note About Inga Moore

Dear Readers,

  "MEEOWW!" That's my way of saying hello. Being the star of a book was hard work. To help Inga Moore write and draw Six-Dinner Sid, I showed her how cats leap, stretch, and purr. She became a real cat expert.

  Did you know that Inga Moore was born in England and moved to Australia when she was seven? Now she lives in London, England.

  When Inga Moore was young, she loved to ride horses. She wanted to be a vet. I'm glad that she became a writer and artist instead so that I could be in her book!

  Hmmm. . . all of this writing has made me hungry. Dinner number one, here I come!

Sid

Response Corner

Six Sides to Sid

Work in groups of six to make a story strip that shows six different sides of Sid.

1. Think about what you liked most about Sid.
2. Draw and write about your idea.
3. When your group has finished, look at all the pictures.
4. Put the pictures in order. Tape them together to make your story strip.

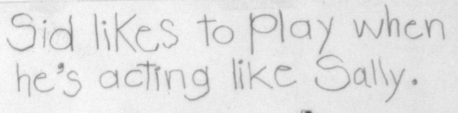

Sid likes to play when he's acting like Sally.

Sid likes to eat fish from a dish.

INTERVIEW A CHARACTER

If Sid Could Talk

You and a partner can make up a TV talk show about Sid. Decide who will be Sid and who will be the host. Plan what you both will say.

BEFORE THE SHOW...

If you are the TV talk show host

- plan the questions you will ask.
- think about what people would want to know about Sid.

If you are Sid

- read the questions.
- think about how a cat might answer.

What Do You Think?

- How is Pythagoras Place different from Aristotle Street?
- If Sid were your pet, which one would you want him to act like—Scaramouche, Bob, Mischief, Sally, Sooty, or Schwartz? Tell why.

201

Rosie *the* Visiting Dog

Meet Rosie. She is a special kind of pet. She visits people to make them feel better.

Rosie went to a special school to become a visiting dog. She learned a lot of things, like how to be patient and never grab at food.

She also learned to be gentle with those who might be rough with her, even though they don't mean to.

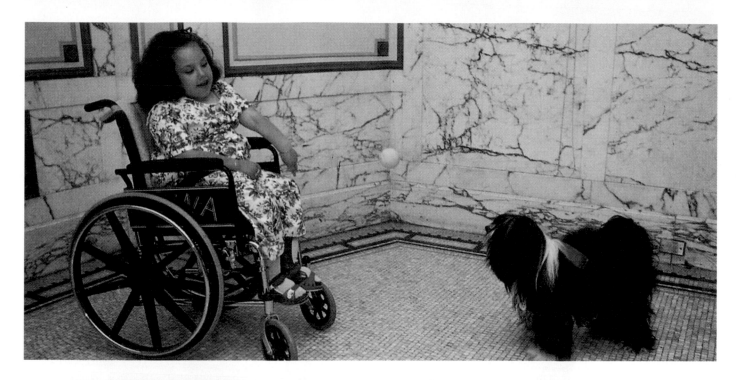

This girl is having fun playing fetch with Rosie.

Sometimes Rosie sits with people who are sad. Her friendship soon cheers them up.

This boy, who is blind, likes to brush Rosie's fur. He loves being with her. So do many other people. Rosie is a good visiting dog—and also a very good friend!

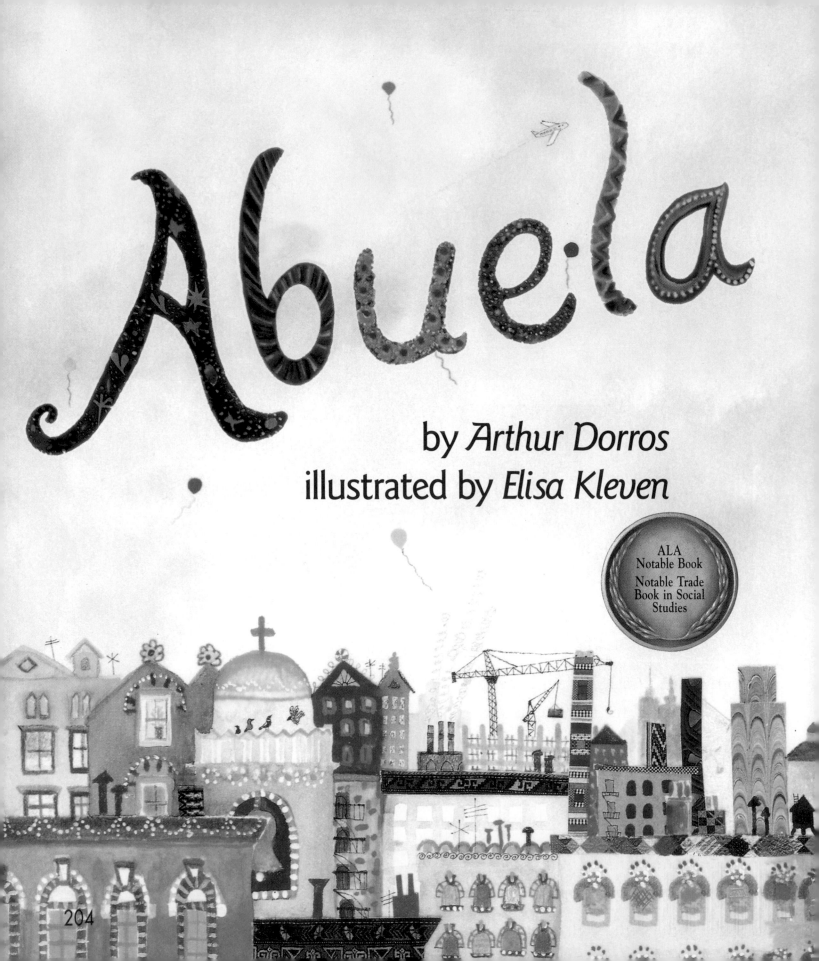

Abuela takes me on the bus.
We go all around the city.

Abuela is my grandma.
She is my mother's mother.
Abuela means "grandma" in Spanish.
Abuela speaks mostly Spanish because
that's what people spoke where she grew
up, before she came to this country.
Abuela and I are always going places.

Today we're going to the park.
"*El parque es lindo,*" says Abuela.
I know what she means.
I think the park is beautiful too.

"*Tantos pájaros,*" Abuela says as a flock
of birds surrounds us.
So many birds.
They're picking up the bread we brought.

What if they picked me up, and carried
me high above the park?
What if I could fly?
Abuela would wonder where I was.
Swooping like a bird, I'd call to her.

Then she'd see me flying.
Rosalba the bird.
"*Rosalba el pájaro,*" she'd say.
"*Ven, Abuela.* Come, Abuela," I'd say.
"*Sí, quiero volar,*" Abuela would reply as
she leaped into the sky with her skirt
flapping in the wind.

We would fly all over the city.
"*Mira*," Abuela would say, pointing.

And I'd look, as we soared over parks and streets, dogs and people.

We'd wave to the people waiting for the bus.
"*Buenos días*," we'd say.
"*Buenos días.* Good morning," they'd call up to us.
We'd fly over factories and trains . . .

and glide close to the sea.
"*Cerca del mar*," we'd say.
We'd almost touch the tops of waves.

Abuela's skirt would be a sail.
She could race with the sailboats.
I'll bet she'd win.

We'd fly to where the ships are docked,
and watch people unload fruits from the
land where Abuela grew up.
Mangos, bananas, papayas—those are
all Spanish words.
So are rodeo, patio, and burro.
Maybe we'd see a cousin of Abuela's
hooking boxes of fruit to a crane.
We saw her cousin Daniel once,
unloading and loading the ships.

215

Out past the boats in the harbor we'd
see the Statue of Liberty.
"*Me gusta,*" Abuela would say.
Abuela really likes her.
I do too.
We would circle around Liberty's head
and wave to the people visiting her.
That would remind Abuela of when she
first came to this country.

"*Vamos al aeropuerto,*" she'd say.
She'd take me to the airport where the
plane that first brought her landed.
"*Cuidado,*" Abuela would tell me.
We'd have to be careful as we went for
a short ride.

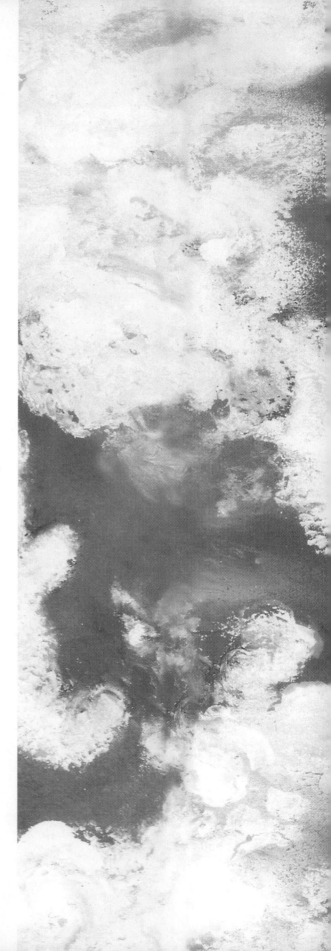

Then we could fly to *tío* Pablo's and *tía*
Elisa's store.
Pablo is my uncle, my *tío,* and Elisa is
my aunt, my *tía.*
They'd be surprised when we flew in, but
they'd offer us a cool *limonada.*
Flying is hot work.
"*Pero quiero volar más,*" Abuela would say.
She wants to fly more.
I want to fly more too.

We could fly to *las nubes,* the clouds.
One looks like a cat, *un gato.*
One looks like a bear, *un oso.*
One looks like a chair, *una silla.*
"*Descansemos un momento,*" Abuela
would say.
She wants to rest a moment.
We would rest in our chair, and Abuela
would hold me in her arms, with the
whole sky our house, *nuestra casa.*

218

We'd be as high as airplanes, balloons, and birds, and higher than the tall buildings downtown.
But we'd fly there too to look around.

We could find the building where my father works.

"*Hola, papá,*" I'd say as I waved.
And Abuela would do a flip for fun as we passed by the windows.

"*Mira,*" I hear Abuela say.
"Look," she's telling me.

I do look, and we are back in the park.

221

We are walking by the lake.
Abuela probably wants to go for a
boat ride.
"*Vamos a otra aventura,*" she says.
She wants us to go for another adventure.
That's just one of the things I love
about Abuela.
She likes adventures.

Abuela takes my hand.
"*Vamos,*" she says.
"Let's go."

Glossary

Abuela (ah-BWEH-lah) Grandmother

Buenos días (BWEH-nohs DEE-ahs) Good day

Cerca del mar (SEHR-kah dehl mahr) Close to the sea

Cuidado (kwee-DAH-doh) Be careful

Descansemos un momento (dehs-kahn-SEH-mohs oon moh-MEHN-toh)
Let's rest a moment

El parque es lindo (ehl PAHR-kay ehs LEEN-doh) The park is beautiful

Hola, papá (OH-lah, pah-PAH) Hello, papa

Las nubes (lahs NOO-behs) The clouds

Limonada (lee-moh-NAH-dah) Lemonade

Me gusta (meh GOO-stah) I like

Mira (MEE-rah) Look

Nuestra casa (NWEH-strah CAH-sah) Our house

Pero quiero volar más (PEH-roh key-EH-roh boh-LAR mahs) But I would like to fly more

Rosalba el pájaro (roh-SAHL-bah ehl PAH-hah-roh) Rosalba the bird

Sí, quiero volar (see, key-EH-roh boh-LAR) Yes, I want to fly

Tantos pájaros (TAHN-tohs PAH-hah-rohs) So many birds

Tía (TEE-ah) Aunt

Tío (TEE-oh) Uncle

Un gato (oon GAH-toh) A cat

Un oso (oon OH-soh) A bear

Una silla (OON-ah SEE-yah) A chair

Vamos (BAH-mohs) Let's go

Vamos al aeropuerto (BAH-mohs ahl ah-ehr-oh-PWEHR-toh) Let's go to the airport

Vamos a otra aventura (BAH-mohs ah OH-trah ah-behn-TOO-rah)
Let's go on another adventure

Ven (behn) Come

The capitalized syllable is stressed in pronunciation.

224

Arthur Dorros

When I was little, I loved to listen to my grandmother's stories. I also thought about flying like a bird. I liked to go up on the roof of my apartment building in New York City. From there, I could see all the places that Rosalba sees when she flies.

When I got older, I married a woman whose family came from Latin America. All the Spanish names in the story belong to members of my wife's family.

Elisa Kleven

Do you like to collect things? I collect scraps of everything, from wrapping paper to yarn. I have special boxes where I store all my scraps. When I do my artwork, first I draw the pictures. Then I fill them in with different scraps.

I enjoyed making the pictures for "Abuela." I even used some material from a blouse of mine to make Abuela's purse.

Response Corner

Come Fly with Me

Draw yourself flying over your home with Rosalba and Abuela!

- Look at the pictures in "Abuela." Everything below looks smaller.
- Plan how you will show your home. Draw your picture.
- Draw yourself flying with the characters from the story.
- Inside a speech balloon, write what you are saying.
  - Share your picture.

EXTEND THE STORY

Another Adventure

On their first adventure, Abuela and Rosalba went flying through the air. They are ready for a new adventure on a boat. Work with a partner. Write what they see and do. Choose a way to share your new story. You might make a book or record your story.

What Do You Think?

- How can you tell that Rosalba and Abuela like being together?
- Would you like to fly with Rosalba and Abuela? Why or why not?

227

THEME WRAP-UP

One of the most important lessons we can learn is how to be a good friend.

- How are the friendships between Matthew and Tilly and between Abuela and Rosalba alike? How are their friendships different?

- Do you think that Sid would be happy to find Mr. Putter and Tabby? Would Tabby be happy living on Aristotle Street or Pythagoras Place? Tell why you think as you do.

Activity Corner

All the stories in this theme are about people and pets that are special to someone. Think about someone who is special to you. What do you most want to tell that person? Write a note to tell your special someone how you feel.

TELL A TRICKY TALE

People all over the world like to tell and to listen to stories. Stories have been passed from storytellers to listeners for as long as people can remember. Some of your favorite stories may have been told over and over for hundreds of years. Other stories may first have been told in faraway places. Stories are something that all people can love and share, especially tricky tales like these.

TELL A TRICKY TALE

Anansi and the Talking Melon

retold by Eric A. Kimmel

Anansi

by Bert Simpson

Tricks Animals Play

by Jan Nagel Clarkson

Nine-in-One, Grr! Grr!

told by Blia Xiong

adapted by Cathy Spagnoli

Art and Literature:
Storyteller Doll

by Michelle Paisano

Coyote

written and illustrated by Gerald McDermott

Secret Messages

by Gordon Penrose

Rabbit and Tiger

by F. C. Nicholson

BOOKSHELF

Two of Everything
retold and illustrated by
Lily Toy Hong

Mr. Haktak finds an old
pot that doubles anything
he puts into it! But when
Mrs. Haktak falls into the
pot, the trouble begins.

Signatures Library

Award-Winning Author

The Rooster Who Went to His Uncle's Wedding
by Alma Flor Ada

Have you ever been late for
anything? A rooster needs
help cleaning his muddy beak
before he can go to his uncle's
wedding. Will he be late?

Signatures Library

Award-Winning Author

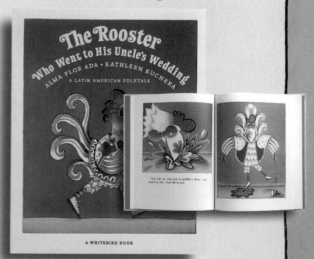

Anansi the Spider
adapted by Gerald McDermott

In this Ashanti tale from Africa, Anansi's six sons save his life.

Caldecott Honor

The Terrible EEK
retold by Patricia A. Compton

In this Japanese tale, a lucky mistake keeps a family safe from a thief and a wolf.

Tops & Bottoms
adapted by Janet Stevens

A rabbit tricks a bear into giving him food from the bear's garden.

Caldecott Honor, Children's Choice

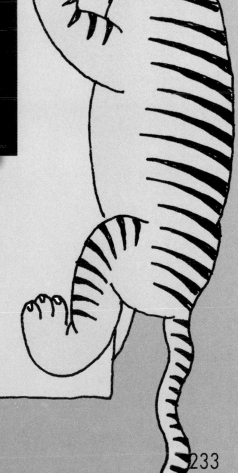

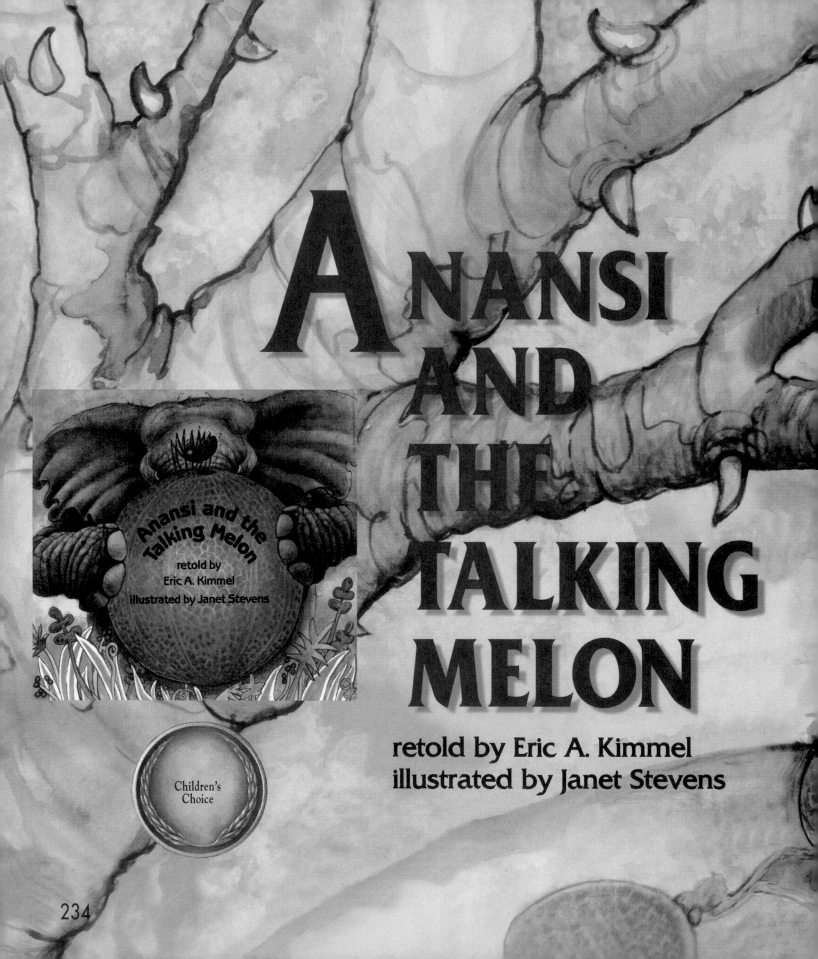

Anansi

and the

Talking Melon

retold by Eric A. Kimmel
illustrated by Janet Stevens

One fine morning Anansi the Spider sat high up in a thorn tree looking down into Elephant's garden. Elephant was hoeing his melon patch. The ripe melons seemed to call out to Anansi, "Look how juicy and sweet we are! Come eat us!"

235

Anansi loved to eat melons, but he was much too lazy to grow them himself. So he sat up in the thorn tree, watching and waiting, while the sun rose high in the sky and the day grew warm. By the time noon came, it was too hot to work. Elephant put down his hoe and went inside his house to take a nap.

Here was the moment Anansi had been waiting for. He broke off a thorn and dropped down into the melon patch. He used the thorn to bore a hole in the biggest, ripest melon.

Anansi squeezed inside and started eating. He ate and ate until he was as round as a berry.

"I'm full," Anansi said at last. "Elephant will be coming back soon. It is time to go."

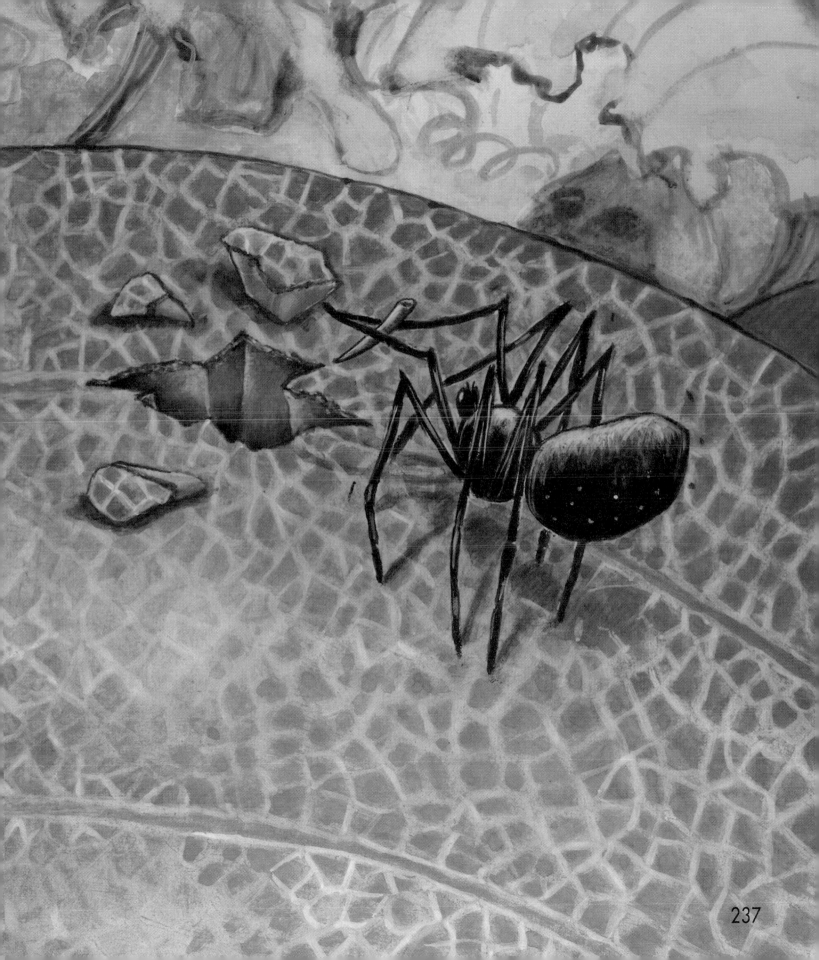

But when he tried to squeeze through the hole, Anansi had a surprise. He didn't fit! The hole was big enough for a thin spider, but much too small for a fat one.

"I'm stuck!" Anansi cried. "I can't get out. I will have to wait until I am thin again."

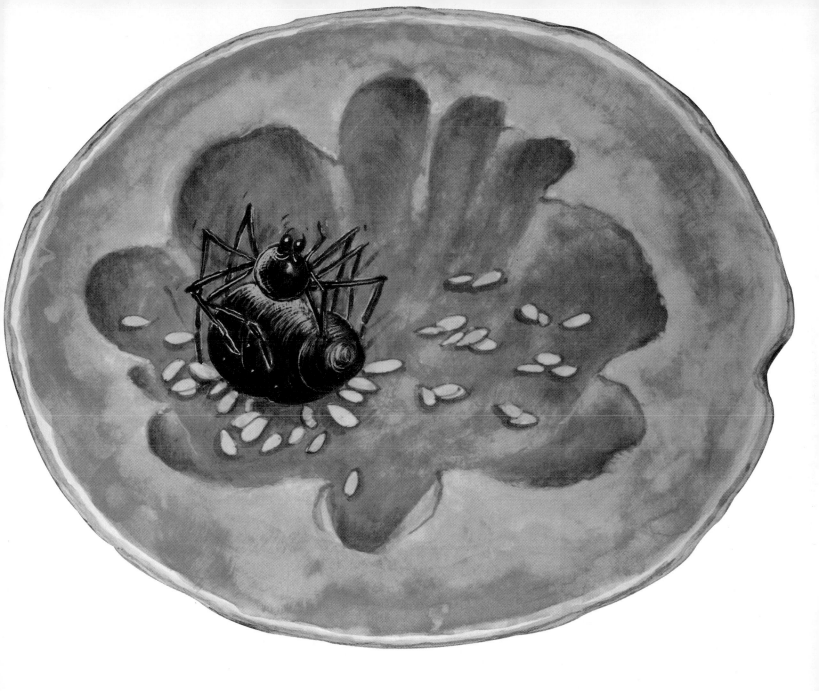

Anansi sat down on a pile of melon seeds and waited to get thin. Time passed slowly.

"I'm bored," Anansi said. "I wish I had something to do."

Just then he heard Elephant returning to the garden. Anansi had an idea. "When Elephant gets closer, I will say something. Elephant will think the melon is talking. What fun!" Elephant walked over to the melon patch. "Look at this fine melon. How big and ripe it is!" he said, picking it up.

"Ouch!" cried Anansi.

Elephant jumped.

"Aah! Who said that?"

"I did. The melon," Anansi said.

"I didn't know melons could talk," said Elephant.

"Of course we do. We talk all the time. The trouble is, you never listen."

"I can't believe my ears!" Elephant exclaimed. "A talking melon! Who could believe it? I must show this to the king."

Elephant ran down the road, carrying the melon with Anansi inside. Along the way, he ran into Hippo.

"Where are you going with that melon?" Hippo asked.

"I'm taking it to the king," Elephant told him.

"What for? The king has hundreds of melons."

"He doesn't have one like this," Elephant said. "This is a talking melon."

Hippo didn't believe Elephant. "A talking melon? What an idea! That's as ridiculous as . . ."

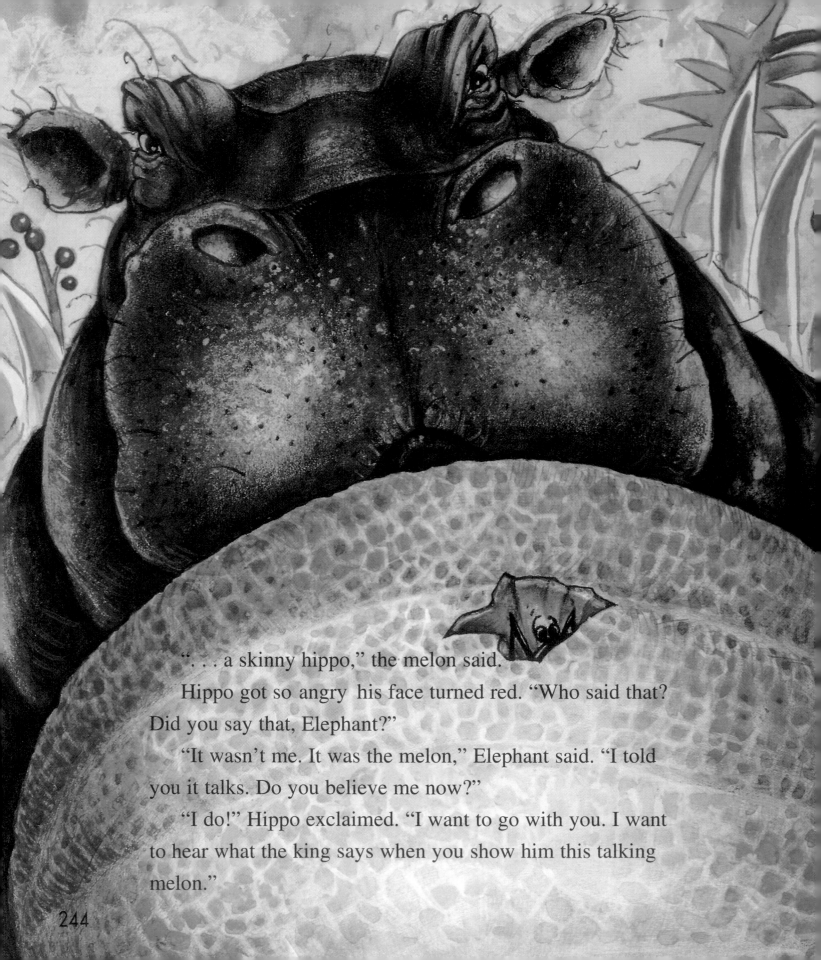

". . . a skinny hippo," the melon said.

Hippo got so angry his face turned red. "Who said that? Did you say that, Elephant?"

"It wasn't me. It was the melon," Elephant said. "I told you it talks. Do you believe me now?"

"I do!" Hippo exclaimed. "I want to go with you. I want to hear what the king says when you show him this talking melon."

"Come along, then," said Elephant. So Elephant and
Hippo went down the road together, carrying the melon.

By and by, they ran into Warthog. "Where are you taking
that melon?" Warthog asked them.

"We're taking it to the king," Elephant and Hippo
told him.

"What for? The king has hundreds of melons,"
Warthog said.

"He doesn't have one like this," Hippo replied. "This
melon talks. I heard it."

Warthog started to laugh. "A talking melon? Why, that's
as ridiculous as . . ."

"... a handsome warthog," said the melon.

Warthog got so angry he shook all over. "Who said that? Did you say that, Elephant? Did you say that, Hippo?"

"Of course not!" Hippo and Elephant told him. "The melon talks. Do you believe us now?"

"I do!" cried Warthog. "Let me go with you. I want to see what the king does when you show him this talking melon."

So Warthog, Elephant, and Hippo went down the road together, carrying the melon.

Along the way, they met Ostrich, Rhino, and Turtle. They didn't believe the melon could talk either until they heard it for themselves. Then they wanted to come along too.

The animals came before the king. Elephant bowed low as he placed the melon at the king's feet.

The king looked down. "Why did you bring me a melon?" he asked Elephant. "I have hundreds of melons growing in my garden."

"You don't have one like this," Elephant said. "This melon talks."

"A talking melon? I don't believe it. Say something, Melon." The king prodded the melon with his foot.

The melon said nothing.

"Melon," the king said in a slightly louder voice, "there is no reason to be shy. Say whatever you like. I only want to hear you talk."

The melon still said nothing. The king grew impatient.

"Melon, if you can talk, I want you to say something. I command you to speak."

The melon did not make a sound.

The king gave up. "Oh, this is a stupid melon!" he said.

Just then the melon spoke. "Stupid, am I? Why do you say that? I'm not the one who talks to melons!"

The animals had never seen the king so angry. "How dare this melon insult me!" he shouted. The king picked up the melon and hurled it as far as he could.

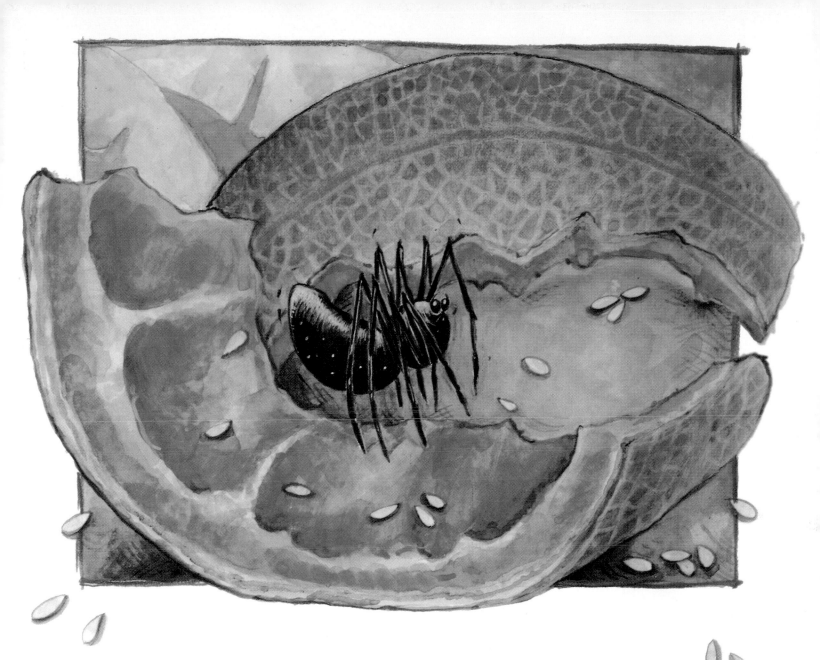

The melon bounced and rolled all the way to Elephant's
house. KPOM! It smacked into the thorn tree and burst into
pieces. Anansi picked himself up from among the bits of
melon rind.

All the excitement had made him thin. And now that he
was thin again, he was hungry. Anansi climbed the banana
tree. He settled himself in the middle of a big bunch of
bananas and started eating.

Elephant returned. He went straight to the melon patch.

"You melons got me in trouble with the king!" Elephant said. "From now on, you can talk all you like. I'm not going to listen to a word you say!"

"Good for you, Elephant!" Anansi called from the bananas. "We bananas should have warned you. Talking melons are nothing but trouble."

Eric A. Kimmel

Anansi and the Talking Melon is a trickster tale that Eric Kimmel has retold. Anansi stories first came from West Africa. They have been passed along to the islands of the Caribbean, to Central America, and to the United States. Each Anansi story teaches a lesson. In some stories, Anansi is a spider. In others, he is a man. But he is always a trickster!

When Eric Kimmel writes, he gets some of his ideas from the mountains, ocean, and deserts near his home on the West Coast. He says that if his wishes come true, he will spend his days on a ranch riding horses and writing books.

Janet Stevens

Janet Stevens has always liked art. When she was little, she thought her sister and brother were better at things than she was. Then she found out that she was good at art and that made her feel happy.

Can you tell that Janet Stevens loves animals? She is well-known for the funny animals she draws in her books. She probably had fun drawing Anansi and all the animals he tricks!

Janet Stevens is married and has two children. She likes to go camping, skiing, and bike-riding with her family.

Anansi

Anansi has a mango tree,
He loves the fruit so ripe.
He cannot reach the mangoes
But he longs to have a bite.

Anansi tells his friend the crow,
"You're beautiful to me."
Old crow calls her friends
So they can hear his flattery.

The crows fly to the mango tree,
They bend the branches down.
Anansi sees them swing and sway
And mangoes hit the ground.

Bert Simpson

illustrated by
Mercedes McDonald

RESPONSE CORNER

Animal Masks

Work in a group. Make an animal mask. Each person in your group can make a mask for a different character from the story.

1. Draw the animal's face on poster board.
2. Cut out holes for your eyes and your mouth.
3. Color and decorate your mask.
4. Tape a craft stick to the back of your mask to make a handle.

Use your masks to act out the Anansi story you just read. Or act out an Anansi story of your own.

You will need:

poster board

markers or crayons

tape

scissors

craft stick

260

I'm Sorry!

Pretend that Anansi is sorry he played tricks on the other animals. He decides to have a party to show them he's sorry. Make a poster that Anansi could use to tell the animals about his party.

Then, share your poster with your classmates.

To make your poster:

• Make up a time and a place for Anansi's party.

• Think about food and games for the party.

• Remember, Anansi is a lazy spider. Think of things he might ask the other animals to bring.

What Do You Think?

• What lesson do you think the animals should have learned?

• What did you like about the story? What didn't you like? Why?

Opossom

Tricks Animals Play

BY JAN NAGEL CLARKSON

TRICKS
Animals Play

The Opossum Plays Dead

◀ HISS! The opossum tries to scare an enemy. If the enemy does not go away, the opossum falls down and plays dead. When it lies very still, it is playing possum. Then an enemy may leave it alone. This is a trick that protects the opossum. Other animals have unusual ways to get food and to keep from being eaten.

Porcupine Fish

These Animals Puff Up Like Balloons

◀ A porcupine fish gulps water when there is danger. It puffs up, and sharp spines stick out all over its body. Do you think another fish will try to swallow a puffed-up porcupine fish?

▶

This lizard gulps air to make its body bigger. And a beard pops out below its mouth. Then the lizard looks so scary it may frighten an enemy away.

Bearded Lizard

Dead-Leaf Mantis

Some Animals Scare Their Enemies With Bright Colors

◄ A red light at the street corner tells you to STOP! The red wings of this mantis seem to say STOP too. Scientists think some animals use bright colors to protect themselves. These bright colors may help scare away their enemies.

◄ The ring-necked snake curls up, and the enemy sees the orange tail.

◄ The bark katydid lifts its wings to show the red color on its back.

◄ As the crayfish gets ready to fight, it shows the red part of its claws.

NINE-IN-ONE, GRR! GRR!

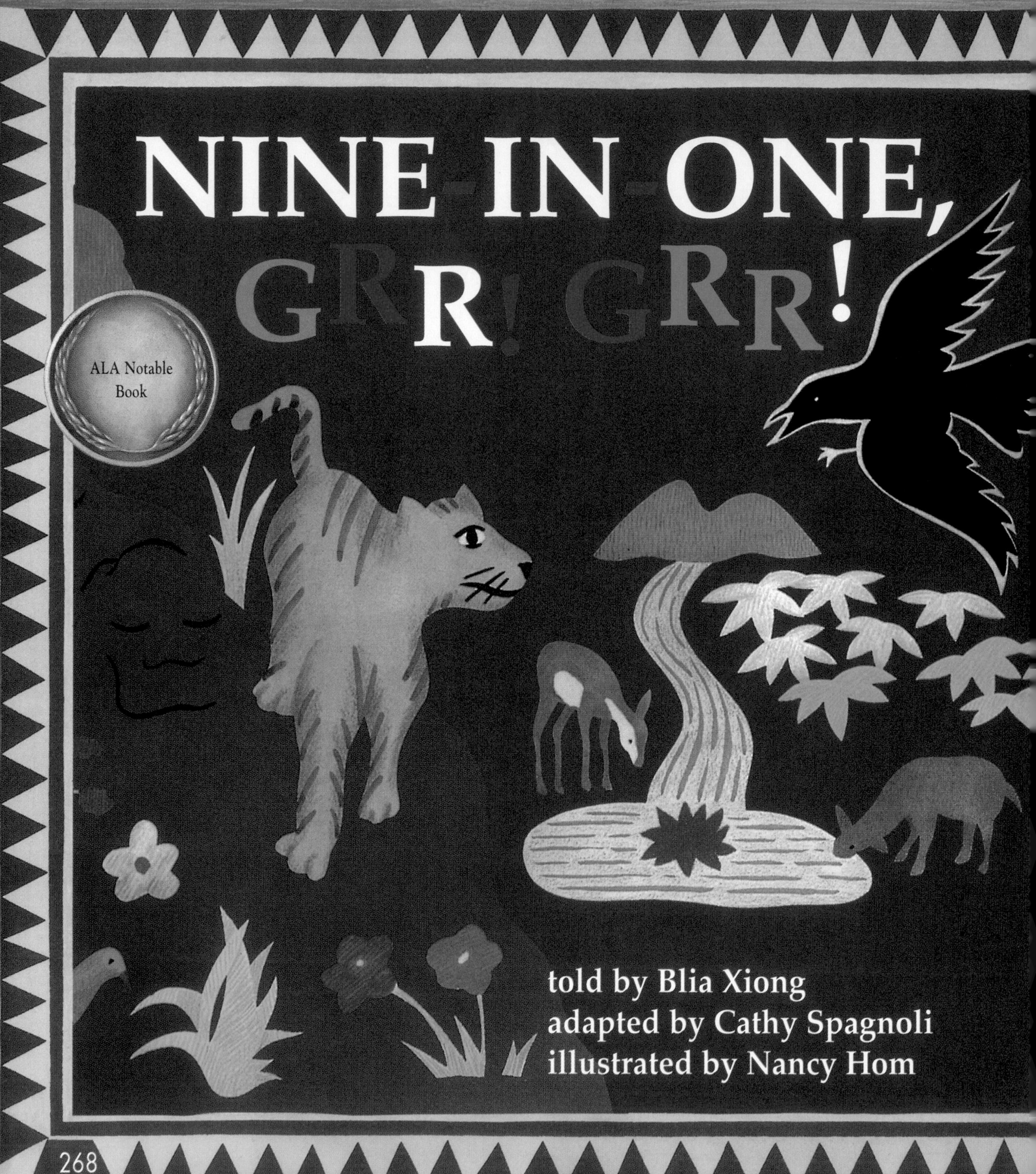

ALA Notable Book

told by Blia Xiong
adapted by Cathy Spagnoli
illustrated by Nancy Hom

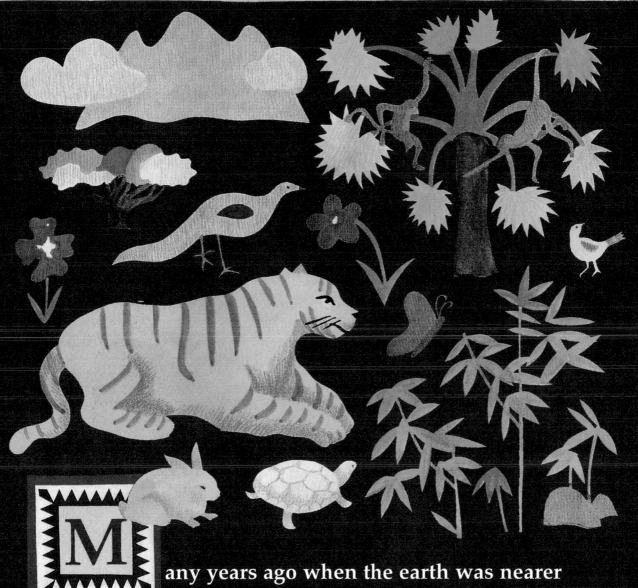

Many years ago when the earth was nearer
the sky than it is today, there lived the first
tiger. She and her mate had no babies and so the
lonely tiger often thought about the future,
wondering how many cubs she would have.

Tiger decided to visit the great god Shao, who lived in the sky, who was kind and gentle and knew everything. Surely Shao could tell her how many cubs she would have.

Tiger set out on the road that led to the sky. She climbed through forests of striped bamboo and wild banana trees, past plants curved like rooster tail feathers, and over rocks shaped like sleeping dragons.

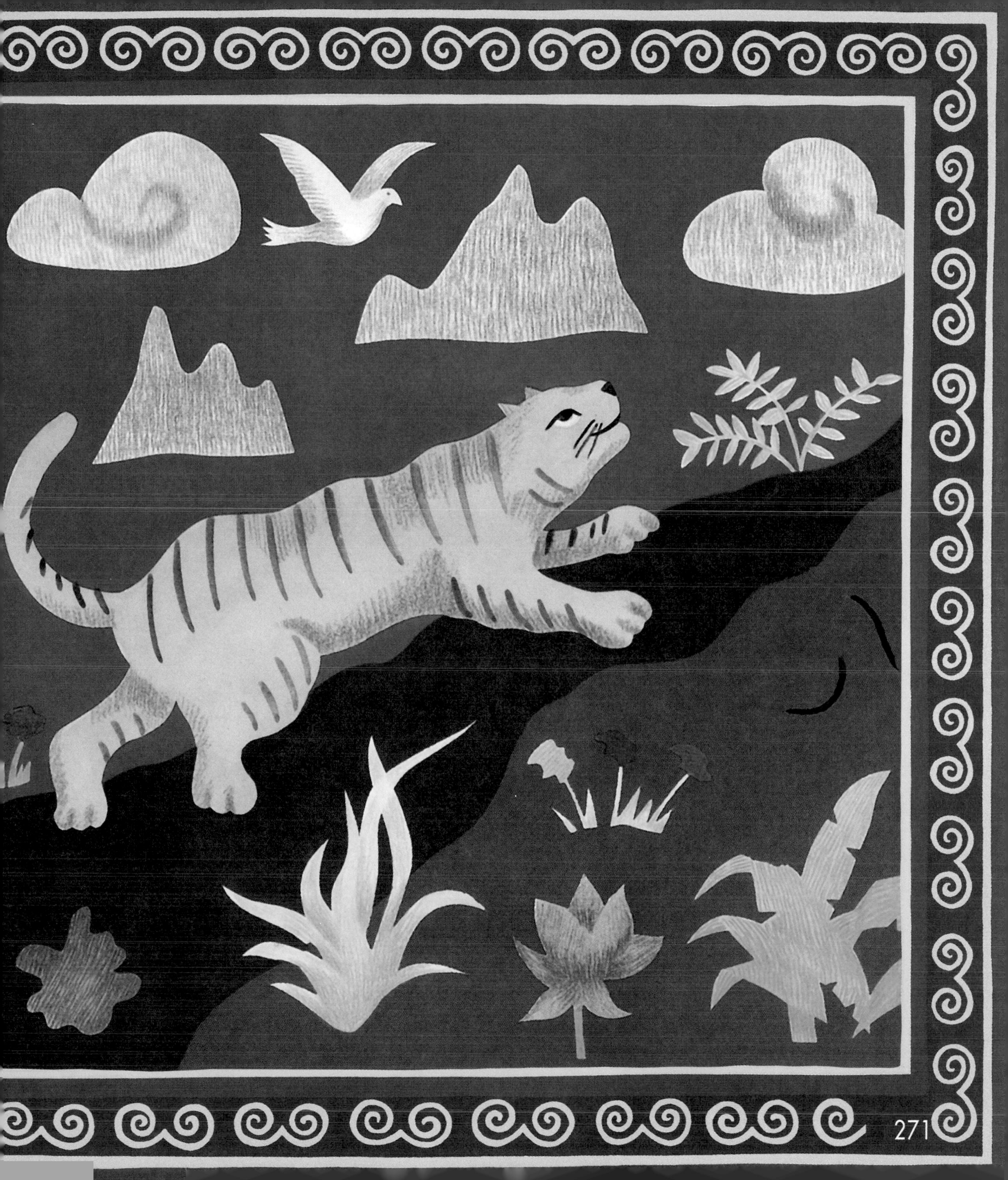

At last Tiger came to a stone wall. Beyond the wall was a garden where children played happily under a plum tree. A large house stood nearby, its colorful decorations shining in the sun. This was the land of the great Shao, a peaceful land without sickness or death.

Shao himself came out to greet Tiger. The silver coins dangling from his belt sounded softly as he walked.

"Why did you come here, Tiger?" he asked gently.

"O great Shao," answered Tiger respectfully, "I am lonely and want to know how many cubs I will have."

273

hao was silent for a moment. Then he replied, "Nine each year."

"How wonderful," purred Tiger. "Thank you so much, great Shao." And she turned to leave with her good news.

"One moment, Tiger," said Shao. "You must remember carefully what I said. The words alone tell you how many cubs you will have. Do not forget them, for if you do, I cannot help you."

At first Tiger was happy as she followed the road back to earth. But soon, she began to worry.

"Oh dear," she said to herself. "My memory is so bad. How will I ever remember those important words of Shao?" She thought and she thought. At last, she had an idea. "I'll make up a little song to sing. Then I won't forget." So Tiger began to sing:

Nine-in-one, Grr! Grr!
Nine-in-one, Grr! Grr!

277

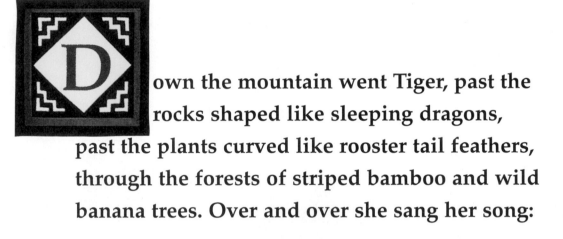

Down the mountain went Tiger, past the rocks shaped like sleeping dragons, past the plants curved like rooster tail feathers, through the forests of striped bamboo and wild banana trees. Over and over she sang her song:

Nine-in-one, Grr! Grr!
Nine-in-one, Grr! Grr!

s Tiger came closer to her cave, she passed through clouds of tiny white butterflies. She heard monkeys and barking deer. She saw green-striped snakes, quails and pheasants. None of the animals listened to her song—except one big, clever, black bird, the Eu bird.

"Hmm," said Bird to herself. "I wonder why Tiger is coming down the mountain singing that song and grinning from ear to ear. I'd better find out." So Bird soared up the ladder which was a shortcut to Shao's home.

"O wise Shao," asked Bird politely,
"why is Tiger singing over and over:

Nine-in-one, Grr! Grr!
Nine-in-one, Grr! Grr!"

And Shao explained that he had just told
Tiger she would have nine cubs each year.

T hat's terrible!" squawked Bird. "If Tiger has nine cubs each year, they will eat all of us. Soon there will be nothing but tigers in the land. You must change what you said, O Shao!"

"I cannot take back my words," sighed Shao. "I promised Tiger that she would have nine cubs every year as long as she remembered my words."

"As long as she remembered your words," repeated Bird thoughtfully. "Then I know what I must do, O great Shao."

Bird now had a plan. She could hardly wait to try it out. Quickly, she returned to earth in search of Tiger.

Bird reached her favorite tree as old grandmother sun was setting, just in time to hear Tiger coming closer and closer and still singing:

> *Nine-in-one, Grr! Grr!*
> *Nine-in-one, Grr! Grr!*

Tiger was concentrating so hard on her song that she didn't even see Bird landing in the tree above her.

Suddenly, Bird began to flap her wings furiously. "Flap! Flap! Flap!" went Bird's big, black wings.

"Who's that?" cried Tiger.

"It's only me," answered Bird innocently.

Tiger looked up and growled at Bird: "Grr! Grr! Bird. You made me forget my song with all your noise."

"**O**h, I can help you," chirped Bird sweetly. "I heard you walking through the woods. You were singing:

One-in-nine, Grr! Grr!
One-in-nine, Grr! Grr!"

"Oh, thank you, thank you, Bird!" cried Tiger.
"I will have one cub every nine years.
How wonderful! This time I won't forget!"

o Tiger returned to her cave, singing happily:

One-in-nine, Grr! Grr!
One-in-nine, Grr! Grr!

And that is why, the Hmong people say, we don't have too many tigers on the earth today!

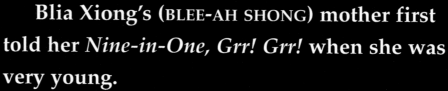lia Xiong

Blia Xiong's (BLEE-AH SHONG) mother first told her *Nine-in-One, Grr! Grr!* when she was very young.

Blia Xiong's family are Hmong (MONG) people who came from the mountains of Laos, a small country near China. Many of the stories she heard when she was young had been told by her family for years.

In 1976, Xiong came to the United States from Laos to get away from the war there. Many other Hmong people from her country came, too. Xiong wanted to help them keep some of their old ways, so she helped start a special club. There, they taught their children music, dance, crafts, and stories like this one from Laos.

Nancy Hom

The pictures Nancy Hom made for this story look like Hmong story cloths. The Hmong people use needle and thread to stitch these beautiful cloths. Each one tells a story.

Nancy Hom used silk screen, watercolors, and colored pencils to make the pictures for this story. Silk screen is done by rubbing different colors of ink through silk onto material or paper.

Nancy Hom was born in the southern part of China and moved to the United States when she was five. Her Chinese background is very important to her. Nancy Hom is married and has a daughter.

RESPONSE CORNER

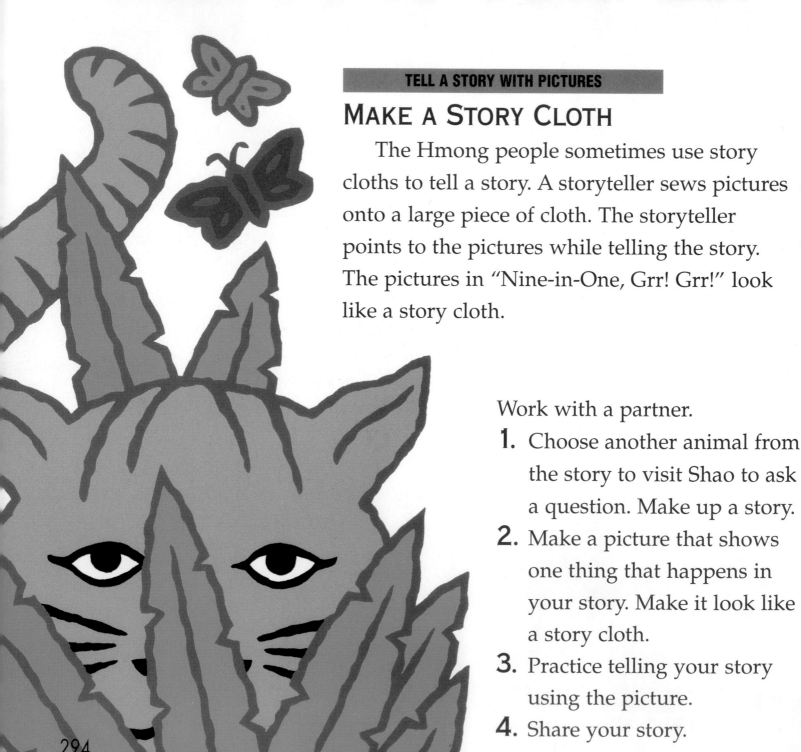

MAKE A STORY CLOTH

The Hmong people sometimes use story cloths to tell a story. A storyteller sews pictures onto a large piece of cloth. The storyteller points to the pictures while telling the story. The pictures in "Nine-in-One, Grr! Grr!" look like a story cloth.

Work with a partner.

1. Choose another animal from the story to visit Shao to ask a question. Make up a story.
2. Make a picture that shows one thing that happens in your story. Make it look like a story cloth.
3. Practice telling your story using the picture.
4. Share your story.

HOW GOOD IS YOUR MEMORY?

In the story, Bird had a good memory but Tiger did not. Test your memory as you play this game.

1. Sit in a circle.

2. The first person says, "On my way to see Shao, I saw a _____ " and names something, such as *tiger*.

3. The next person repeats what was said and adds another thing. That person might say, "On my way to see Shao, I saw a tiger and a mountain."

4. See how long your group's list can get!

WHAT DO YOU THINK?

• Why did Bird make Tiger forget her song?

• Do you think Bird was right to do what she did? Why or why not?

295

ART & LITERATURE

The picture shows a kind of doll, called a Storyteller Doll, that some Pueblo people use when they tell stories. What do you think of when you look at this doll? Could the doll help you tell a tricky tale?

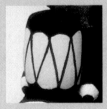

Storyteller Doll
by Michelle Paisano

Long ago, people started making clay dolls like these. They would put the dolls on the floor near them as they sat telling stories. Both the dolls and the stories are a part of Pueblo culture. This doll was made by an artist from New Mexico. It is a mother who is singing a story to her nine children.

COYOTE

A TRICKSTER TALE FROM THE AMERICAN SOUTHWEST

by Gerald McDermott

ALA Notable
Book

Coyote.

Blue Coyote.
He was going along, following his nose.
He had a nose for trouble.

Coyote stuck his nose into
Badger's hole but got bitten.

Coyote wanted to have
a flaming red head
like Woodpecker,
but his fur caught fire.

Coyote went looking for Snake
but only found trouble.

Coyote was always in trouble.

Coyote came to a place where
earth meets sky.
He heard laughing and singing.
He went up to take a look.

Coyote saw a flock of crows.
They were chanting.
They were dancing.

Then the birds spread their wings. They flew through the air and circled the canyon.

"Oh, if only I could fly," said Coyote. "I would be the greatest coyote in all the world!"

Coyote called to the crows.
"Let me join you," he said.

"This foolish coyote wants to be like us,"
Old Man Crow said to his flock.
"Let's have some fun with him."

Old Man Crow turned one eye toward Coyote.
"You may dance with us," he said.

"Thank you! Thank you!" said Coyote.
"But I want to fly, too!"

"Maybe you can," said Old Man Crow.

Old Man Crow plucked a feather from his left wing.
He told his flock to do the same. They stuck the feathers in Coyote.
Coyote winced. His nose twitched.

The crows chuckled.

"You are ready to fly," said Old Man Crow.

The birds began their slow, steady chant. They hopped from one foot to the other. Coyote joined in the dance. Even though he got out of step and sang out of tune, he was very proud of himself.

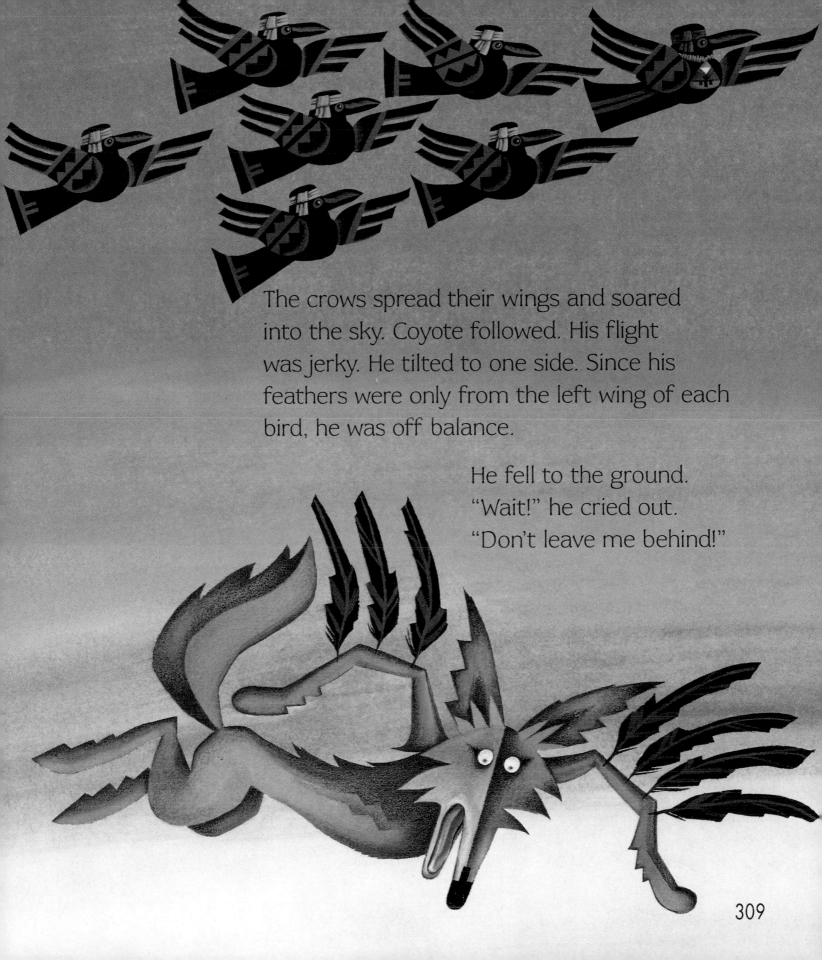

The crows spread their wings and soared
into the sky. Coyote followed. His flight
was jerky. He tilted to one side. Since his
feathers were only from the left wing of each
bird, he was off balance.

He fell to the ground.
"Wait!" he cried out.
"Don't leave me behind!"

The birds returned and gathered round Coyote.
"We must balance him," said Old Man Crow.

310

Old Man Crow plucked a feather from his *right* wing.
Each of his flock did the same. Coyote cringed as they stuck
the feathers in his fur. The crows cackled.

"Now I'm perfect!" said Coyote. "I can fly as well as
the rest of you."

Coyote had become rude and boastful.
He danced out of step.
He sang off-key.
The crows were no longer having fun.

The birds again began their slow, steady chant.
Coyote hopped along, flapping his feathered legs and
singing sour notes.
The dancers spread their wings and leapt into the air.

Soon the crows were flying high over the canyon.
Coyote struggled to keep up.

"Carry me!" he demanded.

The crows circled Coyote
but didn't carry him.
Instead, they took back
their feathers, one by one.

Coyote sank through
the air.

He fell straight down.

"Woooooooooooo!" he howled.

Coyote fell so fast, his tail caught fire.
He fell into a pool on the mesa.

Coyote crawled out of the water.
He heard laughter and saw the crows flying away.

Coyote ran after them.

He tripped and fell,
tumbling in the dirt.

Coyote went home soaked and covered with dust.
To this day, he is the color of dust.
To this day, his tail has a burnt, black tip.

To this day, Coyote still follows his nose.
He has a nose for trouble.
He always finds it.

GERALD McDERMOTT

I have liked folktales since I was a child, especially stories about journeys and heroes. I have spent a lot of time with Native Americans, and their folktales are among my favorites. There are many Native American tales about the trickster, Coyote. This story of Coyote comes from the Pueblo of Zuni. In the Zuni tradition, each of the world's directions has a certain color. The color of the West, where Coyote comes from, is blue. So I made Coyote blue.

Once I have chosen a tale I want to tell, I spend a lot of time talking through the story. I walk around my house saying it out loud over and over. Then, as I write the story, I see the pictures in my mind. I see a dreamscape that comes from my imagination.

319

RESPONSE CORNER

ZUNI HAND MASKS

This story about Coyote was first told by the Zuni people. Some Zuni masks have painted hands on them. Making your hand print is like signing your name. Make your own hand mask.

YOU WILL NEED:
- large paper bag
- scissors
- crayons or markers
- paints and brushes

1. Cut out eye holes and a mouth hole.
2. Trace around your hand. Paint designs in the hand prints.
3. You can use your mask to retell "Coyote."

320

MAKE A FACT SHEET

FACT AND FICTION

This story about Coyote tells why coyotes are the color of dust and why their tails have black tips. Think of why another animal looks or acts the way it does.

You will need:

crayons or markers
books about animals
paper, pencil

Why beavers
have flat tails.
Beavers have flat tails
so they can build dams.
It helps them swim.

1. On one side of a sheet of paper, draw a picture of the animal.
2. On the other side, write one fact about the animal and your ideas about why it is so.
3. Put everyone's fact sheets together to make a class book.

WHAT DO YOU THINK?

- How did Coyote come to be the color of dust and have a black tip on his tail?
- Do you like Coyote? Tell why or why not.

Dr. Zed's Science Surprises

Thirty Experiments For Young Children with Dr. Zed, Star of OWL/TV

by Gordon Penrose
edited by Janis Nostbakken
and Marilyn Baillie

Secret Messages

Send secret messages to a special friend!

HERE'S HOW:

1. Dip a toothpick or cotton swab in lemon juice and draw or print your message on plain paper.

2. Pour salt on the paper to completely cover the message.

3. When the paper is totally dry, brush away the salt.

4. To see the message, rub a pencil or crayon back and forth across the paper several times.

IF YOU WANT TO READ THIS SECRET MESSAGE FROM DR. ZED, HOLD IT UP TO A MIRROR.

For you all :
Here's a message
On your wall
In the mirror
☻ ♡ U !

You can use mirror writing to send a secret message of your own. Simply write from right to left across the page, printing the letters of each word backwards.

RABBIT
and
TIGER

a Puerto Rican folktale
by F.C. Nicholson
illustrated by Richard Bernal

CHARACTERS

RABBIT

TIGER

MOUSE

TOUCAN

MONKEY

TURTLE

SCENE 1

Time: *Long ago. Late morning.*

Setting: *The jungle on the island of Puerto Rico. Toucan, Monkey, and Mouse sit together, talking excitedly.*

Mouse: We can't even get a drink of water from the river because Tiger is always there to chase us!

Toucan: And when I fly into the pongo nut tree, he shakes it so hard I almost fall out. It scares me so much I haven't had a pongo nut in weeks!

Monkey: Just yesterday Tiger curled himself up at the base of the banana tree with one eye open. I didn't dare go near!

Toucan: If only we could get rid of Tiger!

Monkey: But how? We aren't even strong enough to make him stop bullying us, never mind make him go away.

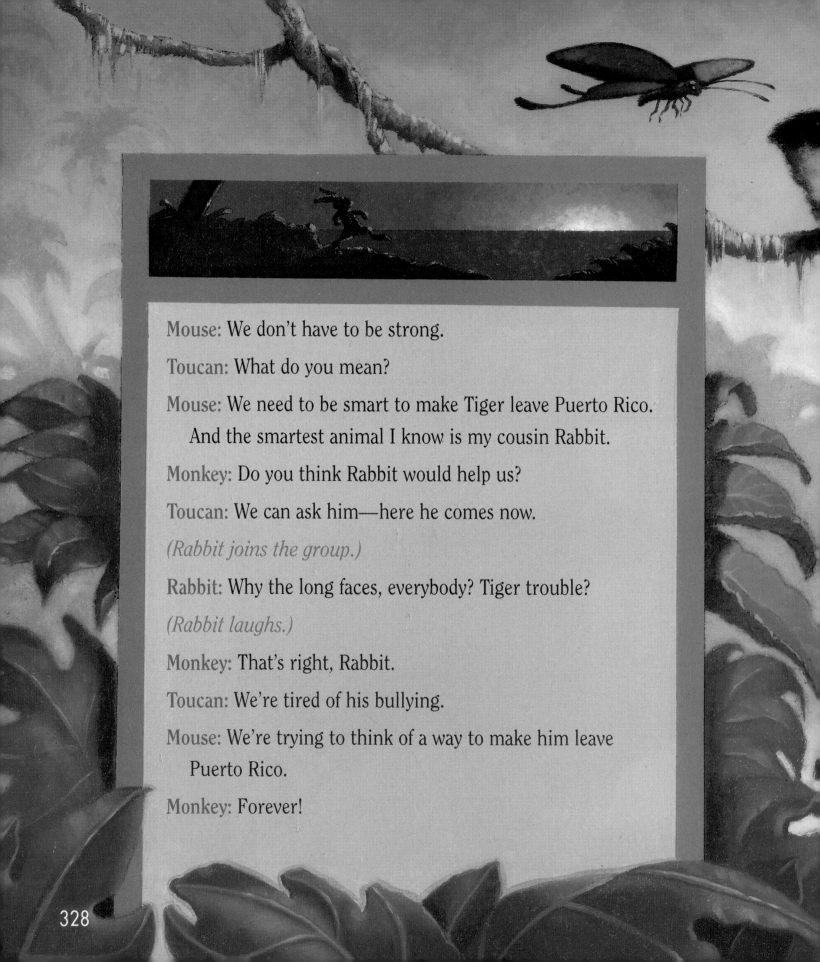

Mouse: We don't have to be strong.

Toucan: What do you mean?

Mouse: We need to be smart to make Tiger leave Puerto Rico. And the smartest animal I know is my cousin Rabbit.

Monkey: Do you think Rabbit would help us?

Toucan: We can ask him—here he comes now.

(Rabbit joins the group.)

Rabbit: Why the long faces, everybody? Tiger trouble?

(Rabbit laughs.)

Monkey: That's right, Rabbit.

Toucan: We're tired of his bullying.

Mouse: We're trying to think of a way to make him leave Puerto Rico.

Monkey: Forever!

Rabbit: Forever, eh? Just leave it to me!

Others: You'll do it? Really? That's great!

Rabbit: My friends, when I am finished, Tiger will never show his striped face in Puerto Rico again!

Mouse: Oh, cousin, thank you!

Toucan: Hooray!

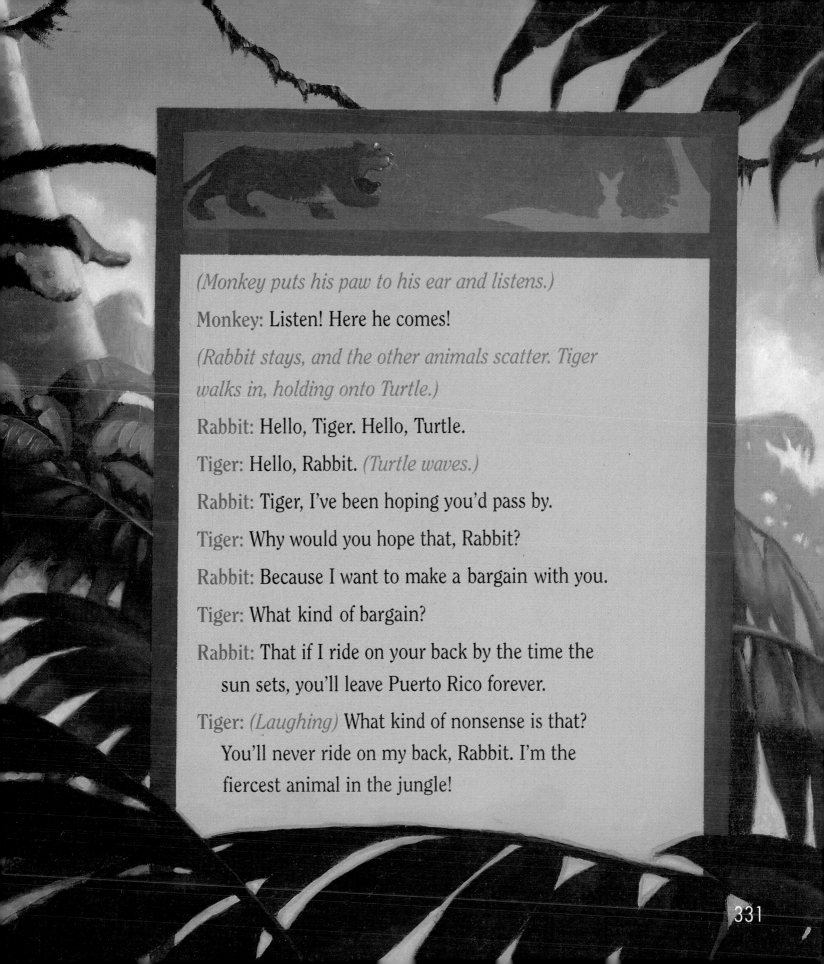

(*Monkey puts his paw to his ear and listens.*)

Monkey: Listen! Here he comes!

(*Rabbit stays, and the other animals scatter. Tiger walks in, holding onto Turtle.*)

Rabbit: Hello, Tiger. Hello, Turtle.

Tiger: Hello, Rabbit. (*Turtle waves.*)

Rabbit: Tiger, I've been hoping you'd pass by.

Tiger: Why would you hope that, Rabbit?

Rabbit: Because I want to make a bargain with you.

Tiger: What kind of bargain?

Rabbit: That if I ride on your back by the time the sun sets, you'll leave Puerto Rico forever.

Tiger: (*Laughing*) What kind of nonsense is that? You'll never ride on my back, Rabbit. I'm the fiercest animal in the jungle!

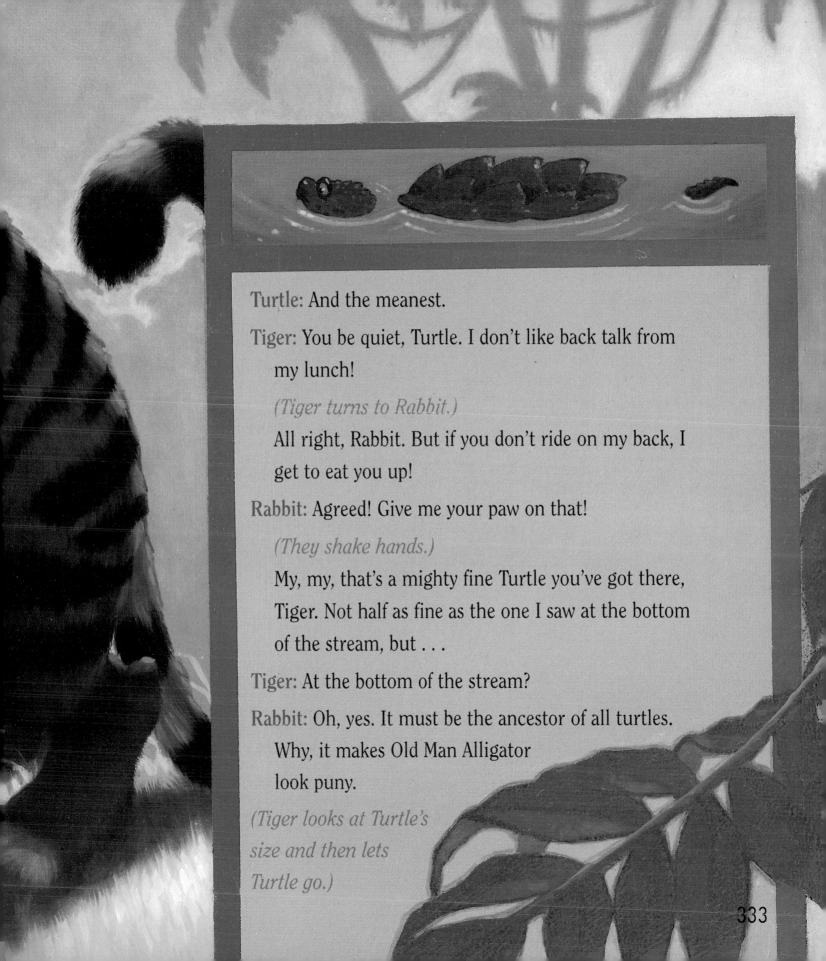

Turtle: And the meanest.

Tiger: You be quiet, Turtle. I don't like back talk from my lunch!

(Tiger turns to Rabbit.)

All right, Rabbit. But if you don't ride on my back, I get to eat you up!

Rabbit: Agreed! Give me your paw on that!

(They shake hands.)

My, my, that's a mighty fine Turtle you've got there, Tiger. Not half as fine as the one I saw at the bottom of the stream, but . . .

Tiger: At the bottom of the stream?

Rabbit: Oh, yes. It must be the ancestor of all turtles. Why, it makes Old Man Alligator look puny.

(Tiger looks at Turtle's size and then lets Turtle go.)

333

Tiger: Such a great hunter as I am deserves such a great lunch. Giant turtle, here I come!

(Tiger leaves.)

Turtle: At the bottom of the stream? But Rabbit, that's where Snapping Turtle lives!

Rabbit: That's right.

Tiger: *(Far away, loudly)* OW!

Rabbit: And it sounds as if Tiger just found out! Come on!

(They hurry off. Tiger comes in, angry, wearing a Band-Aid on his nose.)

Tiger: Just you wait, Rabbit! I'll get even with you! No-good trickster! Nobody makes a fool out of me! I know! I'll go to Rabbit's house and wait for him there! So when he gets home . . . Ha!

(Tiger runs off.)

SCENE 2

Time: *Later that day.*

Setting: *Tiger hides under a table in Rabbit's house. Rabbit comes toward the house, whistling cheerfully. Then he stops whistling and points at the ground.*

Rabbit: Tiger tracks! So, he's inside, eh? Well, I know how to flush him out!

(Rabbit speaks loudly.)

Hello, House! What's wrong, House? You always welcome me home . . . unless there's someone hiding in you!

Tiger: Oh, no! He'll guess I'm in here if his house doesn't answer!

(Tiger speaks in a high, squeaky voice.)

Hello, Rabbit! Welcome home.

(Rabbit puts his paws over his mouth and chuckles.)

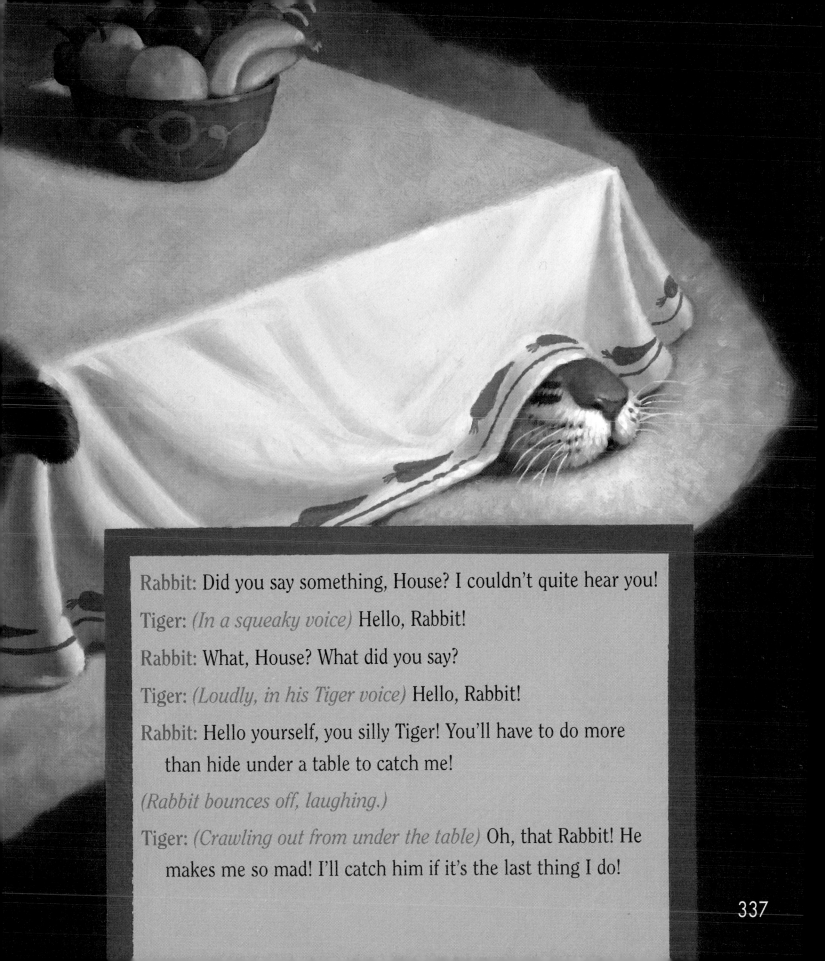

Rabbit: Did you say something, House? I couldn't quite hear you!

Tiger: *(In a squeaky voice)* Hello, Rabbit!

Rabbit: What, House? What did you say?

Tiger: *(Loudly, in his Tiger voice)* Hello, Rabbit!

Rabbit: Hello yourself, you silly Tiger! You'll have to do more than hide under a table to catch me!

(Rabbit bounces off, laughing.)

Tiger: *(Crawling out from under the table)* Oh, that Rabbit! He makes me so mad! I'll catch him if it's the last thing I do!

SCENE 3

Time: *The same day, late afternoon.*

Setting: *Monkey, Mouse, and Turtle are standing around Rabbit, laughing at his story. A long vine is on the ground, nearby.*

Mouse: You mean he really believed that your house talks?

Turtle: But, Rabbit, now that you've made Tiger so mad, how will you ever ride his back? He'll eat you up as soon as he sees you.

Rabbit: Just wait, Turtle. I've got another trick up my sleeve.

(Toucan runs up, excited.)

Toucan: Tiger's coming! Tiger's coming! And does he look mad!

Rabbit: Hide, everybody! You'll get to see Tiger fulfill our bargain.

(Turtle, Toucan, Mouse, and Monkey hide. Rabbit lies down. Tiger comes in.)

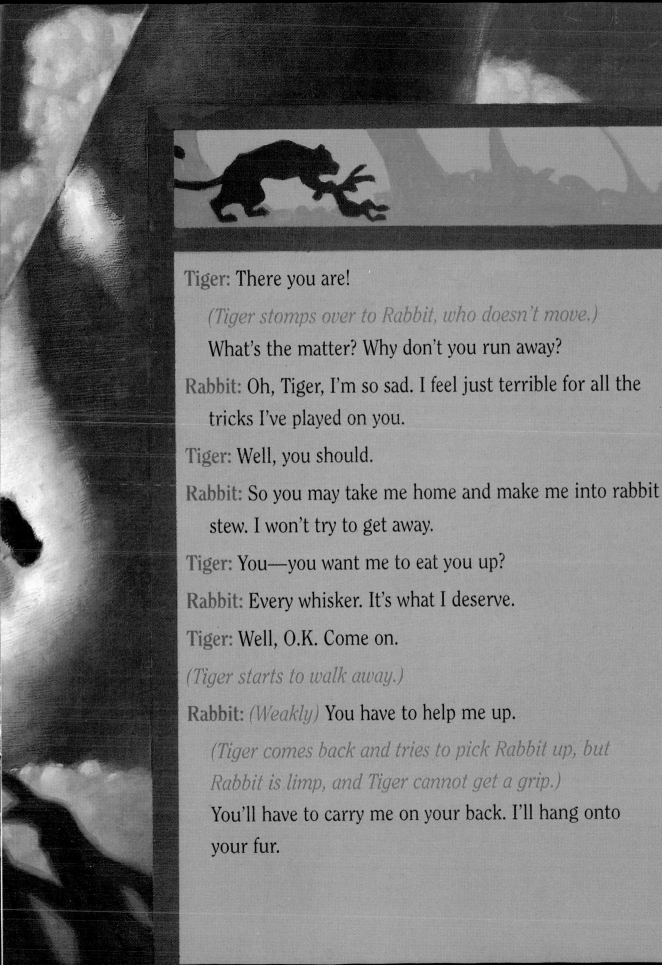

Tiger: There you are!

(Tiger stomps over to Rabbit, who doesn't move.)

What's the matter? Why don't you run away?

Rabbit: Oh, Tiger, I'm so sad. I feel just terrible for all the tricks I've played on you.

Tiger: Well, you should.

Rabbit: So you may take me home and make me into rabbit stew. I won't try to get away.

Tiger: You—you want me to eat you up?

Rabbit: Every whisker. It's what I deserve.

Tiger: Well, O.K. Come on.

(Tiger starts to walk away.)

Rabbit: *(Weakly)* You have to help me up.

(Tiger comes back and tries to pick Rabbit up, but Rabbit is limp, and Tiger cannot get a grip.)

You'll have to carry me on your back. I'll hang onto your fur.

341

Tiger: O.K. Get on, but hurry. I never did have lunch, and I'm hungry.

Rabbit: I can't hang on. Give me a vine to grip.

(Tiger grabs the vine, hands Rabbit one end, and then points to the other end.)

Tiger: What do I do with this?

Rabbit: Hold it in your mouth.

(Tiger puts the vine in his mouth. They move a few steps. Toucan, Monkey, Mouse, and Turtle run in, pointing at Tiger.)

Toucan: Look! Rabbit is riding Tiger!

Monkey: He said he would, and he is!

(Rabbit lets go of the vine. He and his friends laugh. Tiger is angry.)

Rabbit: You gave your word, Tiger! We shook paws on it!

Tiger: You tricked me!

Rabbit: Trick or no, a bargain's a bargain. Now, do you want to walk down to the beach on your own, or shall we carry you?

Tiger: I'm going. I'm going!

(Tiger shakes his paw at Rabbit.)

But someday, trickster! Someday!

Rabbit: Goodbye, Tiger. I hope you're a fine swimmer!

THE END

F.C. NICHOLSON

"Rabbit and Tiger" is a folktale that F. C. Nicholson heard from a friend. Then she saw it in a book and turned it into a play. Ms. Nicholson says, "I liked the story because the smaller, weaker animal comes out on top."

"I read a lot when I was little," she says. "I could read before I went to school. I liked reading stories, and I liked telling them, too. That led me to writing them."

F. C. Nicholson Facts

- The F in her name is for Frances. She is named after her mom.
- She loves animals. She has six cats.
- Of course, she likes to read.
- She likes the outdoors, especially the sea.

F. C. Nicholson

RICHARD BERNAL

I was born in Chicago, Illinois. In the second grade, I liked to draw cartoons. I kept drawing all through elementary school, high school, and then in Art School.

Now I live in St. Louis, Missouri with my lovely wife Catherine and my dog Atticus. I enjoy jogging, hiking, and reading. I also like movies, music, and cartoons. Do you like to go to the zoo? I do! Sometimes when I'm there I draw, and sometimes I just enjoy looking at the animals—animals such as rabbits and tigers!

R. BERNAL

RESPONSE

Puppet Show!

Plan a puppet show for the play "Rabbit and Tiger." Work in a group to make paper-bag puppets. Use the puppets to put on the play.

You will need:

small paper bag
construction paper
scissors
glue
crayons or markers

- Draw your animal's paws, eyes, ears, or beak on construction paper. Cut them out.
- Glue the parts onto the bag.
- After you make your puppets, practice the play. You can perform your puppet play for another class.

CORNER

The Big Cover-Up

What will happen if Tiger doesn't leave the island? Make up a way for Tiger to hide from the other animals. Write a story to tell what happens.

1. Make a painting or drawing of Tiger. Put a disguise on him so he looks like someone or something else.

2. Write a group story about what happens when Tiger tries to fool the other animals.

3. Share your picture and story with classmates.

What Do You Think?

- What kind of character is Rabbit?
- How would you have felt at the end of the story if you were Tiger?

347

THEME WRAP-UP

The stories you've just read have been passed on for many, many years. And they have some of the trickiest characters you'll ever find!

- Which characters in these stories learned a lesson? What lessons did the characters learn?

- In two of the stories, the clever characters are birds. In two of the stories, a tiger is tricked. How else are the stories alike?

Activity Corner

Who is the trickiest character in the stories in this theme? Is it Coyote, or the crows that fooled him? Is it the Eu bird, Rabbit, or is it Anansi? Draw a picture of the character you think is the trickiest one. Write a sentence that tells why.

Using the Glossary

▶Get to Know It!

The **Glossary** gives the meaning of a word as it is used in the story. It also has an example sentence to show how to use the word. A **synonym,** or word that has the same meaning, sometimes comes after the example sentence. The words in the **Glossary** are in ABC order, also called **alphabetical order.**

▶How to Use It!

If you want to find *coins* in the **Glossary,** you should first find the **C** words. **C** is near the beginning of the alphabet, so the **C** words are near the beginning of the **Glossary.** Then you can use the guide words at the top of the page to help you find the entry word *coins.* It is on page 351.

This guide word is the first word on the page.

This guide word is the last word on the page.

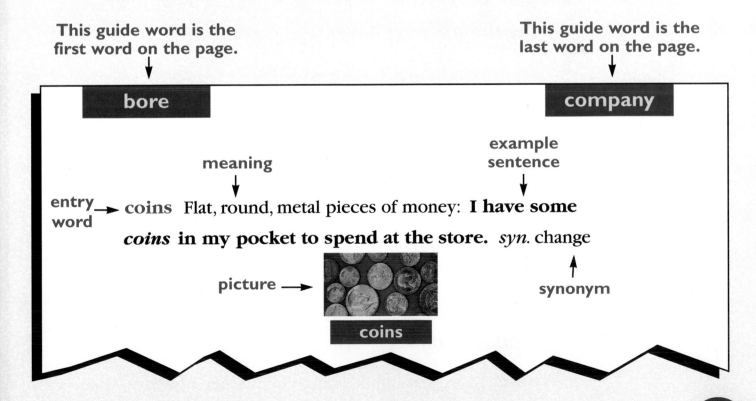

bore   company

meaning

example sentence

entry word → coins   Flat, round, metal pieces of money: **I have some**

coins in my pocket to spend at the store.   *syn.* change

picture →

synonym

coins

349

A

angry

ad•ven•ture A new and exciting thing to do: **It would be a great *adventure* to go to the moon.**

a•gainst To be safe from: **We were dressed in coats *against* the cold wind.**

air The open space above the Earth: **A jet flew through the *air*.**

an•gry Mad: **Did he get *angry* when someone broke his toy?**

ap•peared Came out; could be seen: **The stars *appeared* after the sun went down.**

balance

B

bal•ance Steady; not tilting from side to side: **Susie lost her *balance* and fell down.**

bar•gain A deal: **Rosa made a *bargain* with her brother that she would fix his bike if he would let her ride it.**

beau•ti•ful Nice to look at: **Did you see the *beautiful* painting of flowers?** *syns.* pretty, lovely

be•lieve To trust; to think something is true: **I *believe* that I can learn to swim.**

350

bore To dig into: **You can *bore* a hole through wood with a drill.**

bor•row To use someone's things for a while: **I need to *borrow* a pencil because I forgot mine.**

break To crack into pieces: **Let's *break* the candy into three pieces.**

brought Took along: **I *brought* a sandwich to school for my lunch.**

build•ing A place people make to live, work, or play in: **I watched workers put up a new office *building*.**

bore

building

C

called Said in a loud voice to someone far away: **Tim *called* out "Hello!" to his friend down the street.** *syns.* yelled, shouted

caught Got: **Tony *caught* a cold from his sister.**

change To become different: **Watch the light *change* from red to green.**

coins Flat, round, metal pieces of money: **I have some *coins* in my pocket to spend at the store.** *syn.* change

com•pa•ny Other people or animals to spend time with: **We had *company* at our house for dinner.**

coins

351

coun·try The land where we live: **The United States is a *country* that has fifty states.** *syn.* nation

course Yes: **Of *course* I can help you pick up the toys!**

cous·in A child of an aunt or an uncle: **My *cousin* lives with her dad, my Uncle Fred.**

D

de·cid·ed Made a choice: **Jamal *decided* to go to the park instead of the zoo.**

dif·fer·ent Not the same: **A lion is *different* from a tiger.**

different

dis·cov·ered Found out: **Kathy was surprised when she *discovered* that Tanya likes to play baseball, too.**

E

en·joyed Liked: **Adriana *enjoyed* the song and wanted to hear it again.**

e·nough As much as is needed or wanted: **I have *enough* money to buy three packets of seeds.**

ex·plained Told about: **My dad *explained* how to make a kite.**

F

feath•er Something that covers a bird's body: **The bird lost a blue *feather* from its wing.**

few Not many: **Chen only ate a *few* grapes, so he was still hungry.** *syn.* some

fierc•est Meanest: **The lion is the *fiercest* animal in the zoo.** *syn.* scariest

fool•ish Silly; not wise: **The *foolish* clown tried to drive a car that had no wheels.**

foot The end part of the leg: **Clare put her *foot* into her shoe.**

full Not hungry; filled with food: **I ate until I was *full* and couldn't eat any more.**

fu•ture The time yet to come: **In the *future,* I will become a doctor.**

G

group People, animals, or things that are together: **A *group* of six children played a game.**

feather

fiercest

group

353

H

hungry

heard Took in sounds through the ears: **Mike *heard* the truck before he saw it.**

her•self Done alone by a girl: **Carmen read a book by *herself* after her friends went home.**

hun•gry Wanting something to eat: **The lions are *hungry* because they have not eaten today.**

I

i•de•a A thought: **What a great *idea* to get everyone to help clean the classroom!**

im•por•tant Needing to be done: **She knew it was *important* to finish all her work.**

J

jungle

jun•gle A warm, wet forest with many trees and animals: **The tiger chased the monkey through the thick trees of the *jungle*.**

K

kind Belongs in a certain group: **What *kind* of ice cream do you like?**

knew Was sure: **Suzanne *knew* the movie was good, so she went to see it.**

L

laugh To make a sound showing that something is funny: **That joke made me *laugh*.** *syns.* giggle, chuckle

la•zy Not wanting to work: **Brenda felt *lazy* yesterday, so she didn't clean her room.**

lies To rest your body down flat: **John *lies* on his back to sleep.**

lies

lone•ly Wanting others to be around: **Heidi felt *lonely* in her room by herself.**

loud Making a lot of sound; not quiet: **The music was so *loud* that I covered my ears.** *syn.* noisy

many

M

man•y A lot of: **Carlos got a prize for reading so *many* books.**

mind To think about: **We're so tired that we can hardly walk, never *mind* run!**

mountain

moun•tain A big hill: **That *mountain* is four times higher than this hill!**

N

neigh•bors People who live near you: **I play with my *neighbors* who live next door.**

noise A loud sound: **Did you hear the *noise* that the car horn made?**

P

peo•ple Men, women, boys, and girls: **Many *people* were shopping at the store.**

per•fect Best; just right: **Right before bedtime is the *perfect* time for a good story.**

piece A part of a whole: **John ate a *piece* of pie.** *syn.* part

prac•tice Doing something over and over in order to get better at it: **It takes a lot of *practice* to be a good baseball player.**

proud Feeling good about: **Romulo is *proud* because his picture won a prize.**

pur•ple A color made from mixing red and blue: **Do you like to eat *purple* grapes?**

R

re•mem•ber To think of again; to not forget: **I *remember* the fun we had at the beach last week.**

S

says Speaks: **My mom *says* that I should be nice to others.**

scares Makes someone afraid: **Sometimes the dark *scares* me.** *syn.* frightens

scratched Scraped lightly with fingernails: **Sam *scratched* his bug bite.**

shoes Something worn on the feet: **Yoko will buy new *shoes* because her feet grew.**

shoes

sighed Let out a deep, loud breath: **Laura *sighed* when she could not untie the knot.**

some•times Not all the time: ***Sometimes* I like to wear a hat, but not every day.**

sor•ry Feeling a little bad about something: ***Sorry*, I cannot let you ride my bike.**

sound Something that is heard: **I heard the *sound* of the alarm.**

357

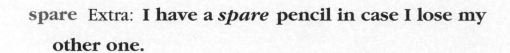

spare Extra: **I have a *spare* pencil in case I lose my other one.**

spe•cial Extra nice; different from the rest: **Alexandra's puppy is *special* because it is the only one with white paws.**

spread To open or unfold; to stretch out: **Alex *spread* his arms as if he were going to fly.**

squeezed Pushed through a small place: **The mouse *squeezed* into the little hole.**

squeezed

start To begin: **Everyone is here, so let's *start* the movie!**

strong Full of power; not weak: **A *strong* wind blew the man's hat off.**

sure Knowing something will happen: **Anya is *sure* she will get a bike someday.** *syn.* certain

T

thorn

ter•ri•ble Bad: **Billy had a *terrible* cold and had to stay in bed.** *syn.* horrible

thanks Something you say to let people know you like what they have done for you: ***Thanks* for your help.**

thorn A hard point on a plant: **Be careful of the *thorn* on that rose!**

touch To reach out and feel something: **Lynn likes to** *touch* **the rabbit because it is soft.**

touch

U

used Did something with: **I** *used* **a stick to stir the paint.**

W

whole All of something: **He ate the** *whole* **thing and didn't leave a piece for me.**

with•out Not having: **If you went out in the snow** *without* **a coat, you would be cold.**

won•dered Wanted to know about: **Mrs. Patel** *wondered* **who was knocking at the door.**

wondered

won•der•ful Great: **Candace had a** *wonderful* **time at the party.** *syns.* terrific, excellent

would Planned to do something: **When she was little, she** *would* **go to bed very early.**

wrong Not right; not correct: **The lock wouldn't open because I used the** *wrong* **key.**

Y

your•self You: **Please help** *yourself* **to some cake.**

359

Acknowledgments

For permission to reprint copyrighted material, grateful acknowledgment is made to the following sources:

Atheneum Books for Young Readers, an imprint of Simon & Schuster: Cover illustration by David S. Rose from *There's a Dragon in My Sleeping Bag* by James Howe. Illustration copyright © 1994 by David S. Rose.

Children's Book Press, San Francisco, CA: Nine-In-One, Grr! Grr!, told by Blia Xiong, adapted by Cathy Spagnoli, illustrated by Nancy Hom. Text copyright © 1989 by Cathy Spagnoli; illustrations copyright © 1989 by Nancy Hom.

Children's Television Workshop, New York: "What's for Lunch? Kids Chow Down Around the World" by Samantha Bonar, illustrations by David Goldin from *3-2-1 Contact* Magazine, March 1995. Copyright 1995 by Children's Television Workshop. "Rosie, the Visiting Dog" from *Sesame Street* Magazine, March 1995. Text copyright 1995 by Children's Television Workshop.

Clarion Books, a Houghton Mifflin Company imprint: Photographs by Justin Sutcliffe from *Rosie: A Visiting Dog's Story* by Stephanie Calmenson. Photographs © 1994 by Justin Sutcliffe.

Dial Books for Young Readers, a division of Penguin Books USA Inc.: Cover illustration by Susanna Natti from *Lionel at Large* by Stephen Krensky. Illustration copyright © 1986 by Susanna Natti.

Dutton Children's Books, a division of Penguin Books USA Inc.: Abuela by Arthur Dorros, illustrated by Elisa Kleven. Text copyright © 1991 by Arthur Dorros; illustrations copyright © 1991 by Elisa Kleven. Cover illustration from *Mary Ann* by Betsy James. Copyright © 1994 by Betsy James. *Matthew and Tilly* by Rebecca C. Jones, illustrated by Beth Peck. Text copyright © 1991 by Rebecca C. Jones; illustrations copyright © 1991 by Beth Peck.

Farrar, Straus & Giroux: "two friends" from *Spin a Soft Black Song* by Nikki Giovanni. Text copyright © 1971, 1985 by Nikki Giovanni.

Greenwillow Books, a division of William Morrow & Company, Inc.: "We Have a New Girl in Class" and "How Do You Feel?" from *Feelings* by Aliki. Copyright © 1984 by Aliki Brandenberg. Cover illustration from *Chester's Way* by Kevin Henkes. Copyright © 1988 by Kevin Henkes.

Harcourt Brace & Company: "The Trade" from *Emily and Alice Again* by Joyce Champion, illustrated by Suçie Stevenson. Text copyright © 1995 by Joyce Champion; illustrations copyright © 1995 by Suçie Stevenson. Cover illustration by Suçie Stevenson from *Emily and Alice* by Joyce Champion. Illustration copyright © 1993 by Suçie Stevenson. *Coyote: A Trickster Tale from the American Southwest* by Gerald McDermott. Copyright © 1994 by Gerald McDermott. *Mr. Putter and Tabby Pour the Tea* by Cynthia Rylant, illustrated by Arthur Howard. Text copyright © 1994 Cynthia Rylant; illustrations copyright © 1994 by Arthur Howard. From "Harcourt Brace Profiles" (Retitled: "Meet Cynthia Rylant") by Cynthia Rylant. Cover illustration from *Tops & Bottoms* by Janet Stevens. Copyright © 1995 by Janet Stevens.

HarperCollins Publishers: "Balloon Tom-Tom" from *Making Music: 6 Instruments You Can Create* by Eddie Herschel Oates, illustrated by Michael Koelsch. Text copyright © 1995 by Eddie Oates; illustration copyright © 1995 by Michael Koelsch.

HarperCollins Publishers (Australia) Pty. Ltd.: Cover illustration by Rod Clement from *Edward the Emu* by Sheena Knowles. Illustration copyright © by Rod Clement.

Henry Holt and Company, Inc.: Cover illustration from *Anansi the Spider* by Gerald McDermott. Copyright © 1972 by Landmark Production Inc.

Holiday House, Inc.: Anansi and the Talking Melon, retold by Eric A. Kimmel, illustrated by Janet Stevens. Text copyright © 1994 by Eric A. Kimmel; illustrations copyright © 1994 by Janet Stevens.

Homeland Publishing, a division of Troubadour Records Ltd.: From "Anansi" by Bert Simpson. Text copyright © 1979 by Homeland Publishing, a division of Troubadour Records Ltd.

Alfred A. Knopf, Inc.: Cover illustration from *Polka and Dot* by Dena Schutzer. Copyright © 1994 by Dena Schutzer.

Little, Brown and Company: From *Dinosaurs Alive and Well!* by Laurie Krasny Brown and Marc Brown. Copyright © 1990 by Laurie Krasny Brown and Marc Brown.

Lothrop, Lee & Shepard Books, a division of William Morrow & Company, Inc.: Cover illustration from *Jimmy Lee Did It* by Pat Cummings. Copyright © 1985 by Pat Cummings. Cover photograph by Ken Heyman from *Puddle Jumper: How a Toy Is Made* by Ann Morris. Photograph copyright © 1993 by Ken Heyman.

Vo-Dinh Mai: Cover illustration by Vo-Dinh Mai from *Angel Child, Dragon Child* by Michele Maria Surat. Illustration copyright © 1983 by Vo-Dinh Mai.

Morrow Junior Books, a division of William Morrow & Company, Inc.: From *Hopscotch Around the World* by Mary D. Lankford, illustrated by Karen Milone. Text copyright © 1992 by Mary Lankford; illustrations copyright © 1992 by Karen Milone.

National Geographic Society: From *Tricks Animals Play* by Jan Nagel Clarkson. Text copyright © 1975 by National Geographic Society.

Plays, Inc.: Rabbit and Tiger by F. C. Nicholson from PLAYS: *The Drama Magazine for Young People*, April 1993. Text copyright © 1993 by Plays, Inc. This play is for reading purposes only; for permission to produce, write to Plays, Inc., 120 Boylston Street, Boston, MA 02116.

G. P. Putnam's Sons, a division of The Putnam & Grosset Group: Cover illustration by Kathleen Kuchera from *The Rooster Who Went to His Uncle's Wedding*, retold by Alma Flor Ada. Illustration copyright © 1993 by Kathleen Kuchera.

Scholastic Inc.: This Is the Way We Go to School by Edith Baer, illustrated by Steve Björkman. Text copyright © 1990 by Edith Baer; illustrations copyright © 1990 by Steven Björkman.

Simon & Schuster Books for Young Readers, a division of Simon & Schuster: Cover illustration by Sheila Hamanaka from *The Terrible EEK* by Patricia A. Compton. Illustration copyright © 1991 by Sheila Hamanaka. *Six-Dinner Sid* by Inga Moore. Copyright © 1991 by Inga Moore. Originally published in Great Britain by Simon & Schuster Young Books. "Secret Messages" from *Dr. Zed's Science Surprises* by Gordon Penrose. Copyright © 1989 by Greey de Pencier Books. *Max Found Two Sticks* by Brian Pinkney. Copyright © 1994 by Brian Pinkney.

Albert Whitman & Company: Cover illustration from *Two of Everything* by Lily Toy Hong. Copyright © 1993 by Lily Toy Hong.

Photo Credits

Key: (t) top, (b) bottom, (c) center, (l) left, (r) right.
Alan Blank/ Bruce Coleman, Inc., 267 (tl,tr); John R. Brownlie/ Bruce Coleman, Inc., 265; Jane Burton/Bruce Coleman, Inc, 264; Stephen Collins/National Audubon Soc., 262; Stephen Cridland/Black Star/Harcourt Brace & Company, 257; Tim Davis/ Photo Res., 265(b); Sal DiMarco/Black Star/Harcourt Brace & Company, 60; Warren Faubel/Black Star/Harcourt Brace & Company, 37(b), 319; Rick Friedman/Black Star/Harcourt Brace & Company, 61, 116, 117; Dale Higgins/Harcourt Brace & Company, 179, 225(r); Ken Karp,118-119, 178-179, 260-261, 320-321; Z. Leszcyndki, 263(b); Tom Myers, 267 (br, bl); Carlo Ontal, 178(c); Edward S. Ross, 266; 267 (cr, cl); Joyce Sangirardi, 146-147; Tom Sobolik/Black Star/Harcourt Brace & Company, 37(t), 91; Justin Sutcliffe, 202-203; Frank Varney/Black Star/Harcourt Brace & Company, 256; Doug Wilson/Black Star/Harcourt Brace & Company, 225(l); Photos from Cynthia Rylant's autobiography "Best Wishes" copyright © 1992 published by Richard C. Owens Publishers, Inc.; Pablo Picasso *Ronde des Enfants* (1901), courtesy of Marc Arthur Kohn, Paris, 64-65; Pierre Auguste Renoir *Two Young Girls at the Piano*, The Metropolitan Museum of Art, Robert Lehman, 156-157; Michelle Paisano *Storyteller Doll*, Museum of the American Indian, 296-297

Illustration Credits

Gerald McDermott, Cover Art; Julia Gorton, 6-7, 13-17, 64, 120; Jennifer Beck Harris, 8-9, 121-125, 156-157, 228; Seymour Chwast, 10-11, 229-233, 296-297, 348; Aliki, 38-39; Richard Bernal, 324-345; Steve Björkman, 18-37; Marc Brown, 96- 117; Samantha Bonar, 42-43; David Goldin 42-43; Nancy Hom, 268-293; Arthur Howard, 158-177, 180-181; Elisa Kleven, 204-225; Michael Koelsch, 94-95; Mary Lankford, 150-155; Gerald McDermott, 298-319; Mercedes McDonald, 258-259; Inga Moore, 182-199; Beth Peck, 126-145; Brian Pinkney, 66-91; Janet Stevens, 234-257, 260-261; Suçie Stevenson, 44-61; Margaret Cusack, 226-227; Sharon Dodge, 294-295; Sudi McCollum 294-295; Scott Scheidly, 118-119 (t), 200-201, 346-347(t); Linda Solovic, 92-93; Peggy Tagel, 62-63; Matt Wawiorka, 40-41.